THIS DELUXE SIGNED EDITION OF

Mediums Rare

[signature: Richard Matheson]

IS LIMITED TO 750 NUMBERED COPIES

This is Number 294

Mediums Rar

Mediums Rare

Richard Matheson

CEMETERY DANCE PUBLICATIONS

Baltimore
❖ 2000 ❖

Cemetery Dance Publications Edition 2000
ISBN 1-58767-007-0

Dust Jacket Art: © 2000 Harry O. Morris
Dust Jacket Design: Bill Walker
Typesetting and Design: Bill Walker
Printed in the United States of America

Cemetery Dance Publications
P.O. Box 943
Abingdon, MD 21009
http://www.cemeterydance.com

FIRST EDITION

10 9 8 7 6 5 4 3 2 1

*To my good friend
Stephen Simon
with gratitude and affection
and great admiration for the
spiritual path he has chosen to take*

Medium: An intermediate agency, means, instrument or channel.

—The Oxford Universal Dictionary

Introduction

This book contains a brief account of psychic beginnings.

Parapsychology, today, utilizes a highly advanced methodology.

It has, long since, left behind the era of dim-lit parlors and spiritual melodramatics.

It is, now, a completely legitimate field of study based upon precise and sophisticated test procedures.

It began quite differently.

Some Early Beginnings

The story about King Croesus of Lydia—somewhere around five forty-six b.c.—is a famous account of the paranormal in ancient times.

As the story goes, King Croesus wanted to declare war on one of his neighboring countries.

He wasn't sure though if he could win or not so he sent envoys to seven of the greatest oracles in the region and had them ask the same question in all seven countries.

"What is King Croesus doing today?" ("Today," being the hundredth day after each envoy had departed from the King.) Five of the oracles got it wrong. The sixth was close. Only the seventh got it right. He spoke about smelling a tortoise and a lamb cooking in a brass cauldron.

Which was exactly what Croesus was doing that day.

Satisfied, King Croesus asked the seventh oracle what would happen if he invaded the neighboring country.

The oracle told him that he saw the defeat of a great army.

Croesus liked the sound of that and invaded.

He should have asked the oracle which army he was talking about.

As it turned out, it was Lydia's.

※ ※ ※

There is good recorded information about a nun named St. Teresa of Avila.

A Sister Anne of the Incarnation at Segovia gave a deposition under oath in which she described how St. Teresa, after kneeling for about fifteen minutes, was raised up in the air more than two feet.

Remaining suspended there for something like a half hour.

※ ※ ※

Emanuel Swedenborg was a Swedish mystic and philosopher of the seventeenth century.

In his earlier years he was a great inventor, designing devices such as a submarine, a flying machine and an air gun that could fire up to seventy rounds without re-loading.

He also wrote important works on astronomy, anatomy, geology and other sciences.

He was, in addition, psychic.

In his later years, religion became his chief pre-occupation.

His most famous book is the *Arcana Coelestia* which he believed he'd received in its entirety from the spirit world.

There is an interesting story having to do with Swedenborg and the widow of the Dutch ambassador in Stockholm.

A goldsmith came to see her some time after her husband had died and asked to be paid for a silver service her husband had bought from him.

The wife was sure her husband had already paid the bill but couldn't prove it.

As the amount was considerable, she asked Swedenborg for his help.

He came to her house three days after her request and told her that he'd had a conversation with her late husband.

He said that the bill *had* been paid and that the receipt for it was in a certain bureau in an upstairs room.

The widow was embarrassed by this because she knew that the bureau had been entirely cleaned out.

Swedenborg told her that the top left hand drawer of the bureau should be removed to reveal a board which, when drawn out, would reveal a secret compartment and the missing receipt as well as some letters.

They went upstairs and found the compartment exactly as Swedenborg had described it. The receipt was there. So were the letters.

※ ※ ※

Swedenborg also described a fire in Stockholm when he was in Gothenburg, three hundred miles away.

He told a group of fifteen people how a house that belonged to a friend of his was in ashes and that his own house was in danger. About four hours later, he told the group that the fire was out, extinguished only three doors from his house.

This all took place on a Saturday afternoon.

On Sunday, Swedenborg described the fire to the local governor—how it began, how long it had burned and how it had been put out.

On Monday evening, a messenger arrived from Stockholm.

The letters he carried described the fire exactly as Swedenborg had on the previous Saturday and Sunday.

✳ ✳ ✳

A few years after the philosopher Immanuel Kant had described Swedenborg's clairvoyant powers—(the power to see at a distance), the first official inquiry into paranormal phenomena was conducted in France.

It was designed specifically to investigate the claims of one Anton Mesmer, an Austrian doctor who claimed that he was healing people with a force he called 'animal magnetism.' (Later to be called 'Mesmerism.')

Mesmer's consulting rooms were illuminated most mysteriously, hung with mirrors, heavily perfumed. Soft music played while Mesmer wandered around among his patients, dressed in a violet robe and carrying an iron wand.

The main feature of the room was an apparatus called a *baquet*, a circular wooden tub filled with water, iron filings and what Mesmer chose to call 'magnetized' water.

Patients sat around the tub, linked together with wet ropes. Iron rods—Mesmer called them 'conductors'—extended from the tub and were placed in contact with the affected parts of each patient.

Up to thirty rods were utilized simultaneously, creating a mild electric current since the tub was like a Leyden jar, a forerunner of the battery.

Mesmer and his assistants would stroke the patients and make strange, ritual-like hand movements over them and Mesmer would touch them with his iron wand.

This, added to the electrical stimulation, would cause the patients to get excited and, usually, end up having convulsions.

Naturally, having that many patients together at one time contributed to a kind of contagious hysteria.

It was no wonder, then, that so many of these people were convinced that they were healed.

Mesmerism also resulted in sleep-like states during which patients demonstrated an ability at paranormal self-diagnosis and, on more than one occasion, telepathy, clairvoyance and prediction.

In the eighteen forties, a surgeon named James Braid experimented with Mesmerism and coined the word 'neuro-hypnosis' which was later shortened to 'hypnosis.'

❋ ❋ ❋

While not exactly an account of mediumship, it is interesting to note that many of the founders of the United States government were Masons. It has even been suggested that they received aid from some secret organization in Europe which helped to establish the United States for some specific purpose known only to an initiate few.

At any rate, the Great Seal of the United States is the signature of this organization and the unfinished pyramid with the All-Seeing Eye hovering over it, on the other side of the bill, is a symbol of the task to which the United States government was dedicated.

Analysis of the Great Seal reveals a mass of occult and Masonic symbols. The eagle was, as a matter of fact, a *phoenix* on the original design, with the Great Pyramid of Gizeh on the reverse side. On a colored sketch submitted by William Barton in 1783, an actual phoenix appears sitting on a nest of flames, a symbol of the new rising from the old.

Later, both of these illustrations were altered to what they are today. Benjamin Franklin thought the eagle was unworthy to be chosen as the emblem of a great, progressive nation, saying that it "was not even a bird of good moral character." He suggested the turkey.

❋ ❋ ❋

The significance of the mystical number thirteen is not limited to the number of the original colonies either. It appears frequently on the Great Seal as well. For instance, the sacred emblem which appears above the head of the eagle contains thirteen stars. The motto *E. Pluribus Unum* contains thirteen letters. So, too, does the description *Annuit Coeptis* on the reverse side of the bill. The eagle clutches, in its right talon, a branch bearing thirteen leaves and thirteen berries. And, in its left talon, it carries a sheaf of thirteen arrows. An interesting side-note to this is the fact that the head of the eagle faces *away* from the arrow of war, toward the branch of peace.

Then too, the face of the now unfinished pyramid, exclusive of the bottom panel with the date on it, consists of seventy-two stones arranged in thirteen rows.

❋ ❋ ❋

Returning to mediumship.

It is generally accepted that the birth of Spiritualism (which was, in time, the origin of modern Parapsychology) took place in the home of Mr. and Mrs. John D. Fox in the year 1848.

The Fox Sisters

March 31, 1848
Hydesville, New York

Since they'd moved into the house the previous December, noises had been bothering them.

The farm house was a small one, consisting of a single floor with several rooms, a cellar underneath it and a loft above.

Rappings and sounds like that of moving furniture had been heard time and again.

John David Fox and his wife had lit candles and moved around the house, searching every room.

They'd never discovered a source of the noises.

This night, they were worse than they had ever been, occurring in all parts of the house.

The couple even thought they heard footsteps in the pantry and Margaret Fox was sick with fear, convinced that some unhappy spirit haunted the house.

It had snowed that day and an icy wind was scouring the house. John Fox kept checking the sashes on the windows, thinking that they might be rattling to cause the sounds.

But the noises were taking place everywhere and both he and his wife were frightened for their two daughters, Margaret, ten, and Kate, seven; the two girls slept in the same room with them.

In an attempt to rationalize the fear they were experiencing, the girls had begun to attribute the noises to some mysterious, invisible entity named Mr. Splitfoot.

Their parents weren't happy with this fancy but allowed it to persist since it seemed to ameliorate the girls' reaction to the noises. And there was certainly no way they could afford to leave the house.

They would all have to make the best of this disturbing situation.

Mr. Fox had not yet retired that night; it wasn't even seven o'clock. His wife lay awake in bed, her daughters lying equally awake in their adjoining bed.

The loud, rapping noises were almost constant now, sounding from every quarter of the house.

Once the beds both jarred, making Mrs. Fox and their daughters gasp in shock.

Abruptly, Kate, her body locked with dread, cried out impulsively, "Mr. Splitfoot, do as I do!" and suddenly began to clap her hands.

The noises seemed to imitate and follow her until she stopped.

A heavy silence fell, mother and daughters wide-eyed, heart-beats thumping.

Then Margaret cried out brazenly, "No, do just as *I* do!" and clapped her hands four times, calling, "Count one, two, three, four!"

Four rapping sounds immediately followed.

The younger Margaret shivered, pulling up the covers to her chin, her face gone pale.

What had she *done*?

She caught her breath, glancing sharply at her younger sister as Kate spoke, saying, "Mother, I know what it is. Tomorrow is April-fool day and it's somebody trying to fool us."

Mrs. Fox felt otherwise, convinced that someone haunted their house.

Her voice trembled while she asked, as proof, for the spirit to rap out the ages of her children.

Ten distinct rap sounds in the small room. Silence for a moment or two. Then seven raps. Kate whimpered, "*Oh.*"

Silence. Then three more raps were heard. Mrs. Fox sobbed frightenedly.

There'd been another daughter who had died at the age of three.

"Is this a human being who answers my questions so correctly?" she asked in a feeble voice.

Silence. Her two girls clung to one another.

Mrs. Fox's throat moved as she swallowed with difficulty. "Is it a *spirit*?" she asked. "If it is, make two raps."

Two rapping noises sounded instantly, causing them to cry out.

Mr. Fox was in the same room now, listening, his expression tense.

"If it's an *injured* spirit, make two raps," said his wife.

The two raps were so loud, the house trembled from the impact. "Dear God," whispered John Fox.

Then he cried out, "Will you continue to rap if I call in my neighbors so they can hear it too?!"

Again, the house shook with the violence of the answering raps.

❋   ❋   ❋

At half past seven, Mr. Fox brought back their nearest neighbor, Mrs. Redfield.

Having heard his rambling account of what had happened, Mrs. Redfield was prepared to laugh, thinking it a joke.

But the moment she saw Dr. Fox and the two girls in their beds, pale with fright, she realized that something serious was happening.

"Ask it who it is," Mrs. Fox told her. She had already done so and wanted to find out if Mrs. Redfield got the same answers she did.

Mrs. Redfield began to do this, asking one rap for yes and two for no.

By this gradual method, she discovered that the spirit was that of a man aged thirty-one, a peddler who had been murdered in this house, his remains buried in the cellar.

It was precisely what Mrs. Fox had been told by the rapping noises.

Mrs. Redfield then went out and got Mr. Fuesler and his wife who, in turn, got Mr. and Mrs. Hyde and Mr. and Mrs. Jewell.

All of them asked the same questions using one rap for yes and two for no.

The answers remained the same. A man. Thirty-one. Peddler. Murdered. Remains buried in the cellar.

The questioning continued through the night, long after the two girls had fallen asleep from exhaustion.

The story grew more bizarrely complicated by the hour.

The murder was committed in the east bedroom five years earlier.

On a Tuesday at midnight.

The victim had had his throat cut with a butcher knife after which his body had been dragged through the pantry and down the stairway to the cellar where it was buried ten feet under the ground.

The murder had been committed to get the man's money. Five hundred dollars in all.

※　※　※

They started digging in the cellar the next night but soon had to give up because they came to water. They could not resume until summer.

Then, at a depth of five feet, they found a wooden plank. Beneath the plank was charcoal and lime, hair and bones.

Doctors pronounced them to be the remains of a human skeleton.

※　　※　　※

Soon afterward, the phenomena assumed the character of a full-fledged haunting.

The sound of a death struggle was heard. A hideous throat gurgling, then dragging of a body across the floor of the house.

The sound of digging in the cellar.

Mrs. Fox's hair began to turn white and, at last, the family had to leave the house.

The raps continued after they were gone.

One night, more than three hundred people conversed with the invisible entity.

※　　※　　※

Kate was sent to the house of an older brother, Margaret to the house of her older sister.

The phenomena continued in both places.

It was especially severe where Margaret was.

Her older sister was exposed to the first recorded "poltergeist" episode in the United States, objects hurled at her, pins stuck into her as she prayed, her cap and combs jerked roughly from her head.

One night, a visiting friend attempted to converse with the rambunctious spirit and, with deafening raps, a message was spelled out: "Dear friends, you must proclaim this truth to the world. This is the dawning of a new era. You must not try to conceal it any longer."

AFTERWARD

Margaret Fox recanted in her later years.

She claimed that she and her sister Kate had produced the rappings by cracking their toe joints.

Eminent physiologist and Nobel laureate Charles Richet—who was involved in psychical research for more than thirty years—had this to say about Margaret Fox's recantation.

"Can we suppose that two children—seven and ten years of age—organized a fraud that succeeded in spite of being tested thousands of times?"

It was a fact that both Fox sisters became alcoholics in their later years. It would have, therefore, been relatively simple for their enemies to persuade them to publicly recent and denounce Spiritualism.

❇   ❇   ❇

In the year 1904, in what had been the farm house of the Fox family, part of a cellar wall fell down.

Revealing an almost entire human skeleton.

Near the skeleton was the tin box of a peddler.

INTERIM

Following the events at Hydesville, all manner of physical phenomena began to appear across the country.

Spirit voices were heard in séance rooms.

Spirit forms materialized in whole or part.

Spoken and written spirit teachings began to wildfire across America, all attributed to eminent—no longer living, of course—men of the past.

By 1853, it was estimated that there existed, in the state of New York alone, some forty thousand Spiritualists.

Despite widespread denunciation from the press, the movement flourished and continued to grow.

Mediums appeared everywhere and, owing to the ever-mounting demand for sittings, the numbers of professional mediums increased proportionately.

It was not professional mediumship which popularized the cause however.

Table tilting at home became the rage in all parts of the country as well as in England and on the Continent.

Tables tilted and rotated and made all kinds of movements without any signs of visible control, every movement interpreted as evidence of questions answered from "The Other Side."

Spiritualism, despite attempts to establish it as a form of legitimate philosophy, came primarily to designate a religious sect. The doctrine of this sect was that spirits of the dead survive as individual personalities and can be communicated with through persons known as mediums.

It also came to be accepted that these mediums could cure diseases with the aid of so-called Spirit Guides or Controls.

Likewise, it became a conviction among adherents that mediums could counsel their clients on a wide range of personal and practical matters, drawing upon the knowledge of the Spirit World.

Also assumed to be a part of mediumship was clairvoyance (knowledge of hidden or distant events) and the ability to predict the future.

Soon, a wave of fascination regarding Spiritualism spread across the Western world, the number of believers in the new faith mounting to ten million.

Nor were all of these disciples limited to the ranks of the uneducated and credulous. Distinguished men from every walk of life became numbered among its converts. Alfred Russel Wallace, the eminent biologist and, later, Sir William Barrett, Sir William Crookes and Sir Oliver Lodge were among the noted scientists whose names became associated with the cause.

Even a president of the United States.

Nettie Colburn

December 17, 1862
Washington, D.C.

The closed carriage rattled through the darkened, cobble-stone streets, inside of it Nettie Colburn and a friend of hers named Mr. Laurie.

Twenty years of age, Nettie was a pretty young woman, attractive to all men who saw her.

Tonight, she would not have drawn a glance, however, unless it was one of pity, her eyes and nostrils red and swollen from days of crying.

"Will he help me?" she asked. "*Will* he, Mr. Laurie?"

"I can think of no one else who could help you more," he replied.

"Yes, but will he? *Will* he?"

Nettie sobbed and dabbed the damp ball of her handkerchief against her sore eyes.

"If my brother isn't furloughed from that awful hospital, he'll die. I *know* he'll die."

"Shh." Mr. Laurie took her left hand in both of his and pressed it reassuringly. "Alexandria is not that far away. It is not that difficult a problem to repair."

"He's so desperately ill though," Nettie said. "He must be furloughed home. He *must* be."

"I understand," Mr. Laurie replied. "That is why we're here."

She nodded, drawing in tremulous breath. "Please God he will help us," she murmured.

The carriage stopped, her breath catching with alarm.

"We're *here*," she whispered.

The carriage door was opened by a soldier who assisted Nettie down to the walkway. Mr. Laurie followed and showed an officer the letter of permission.

The officer nodded and the two were ushered through a doorway on each side of which an armed soldier stood on guard.

Their footsteps made no more than faint clicking sounds in the high-ceilinged corridors through which they were escorted by the soldier.

Nettie Colburn's face was tense with apprehension as they walked along the dimly lit hallways.

What if he could *not* help her brother? If *he* could not, all hope was lost.

At last, they reached a door which the soldier opened, gesturing for them to enter.

The parlour before them was cheerily lit by oil lamps, firelight and candles.

Nettie was surprised to see, waiting for them, Mr. Laurie's daughter Mrs. Miller, Mr. Newton and—

Her breath faltered as she caught sight of the small woman standing by the fireplace, looking at her.

His *wife*, she thought. She had not expected to see *her*.

"Good evening, my dear," said Mrs. Lincoln.

Nettie barely felt Mr. Laurie's supporting hand on her arm as he guided her into the Red Parlour of the White House.

Mr. Newton, the Secretary of the Interior, stepped forward to greet her, taking both her hands in his. "Miss Colburn," he said.

He looked concerned. "Your hands are very cold."

Nettie smiled politely. "Yes, sir. It is cold outside."

"Come over by the fire, my dear," Mrs. Lincoln told her.

Nettie did as she was told and Mrs. Lincoln gripped her right hand firmly. "Oh, you *are* cold," she said, her voice distressed.

She gestured toward the crackling fire and, obediently, Nettie extended the palms of her hands to the pulsing radiations of heat.

"That feels good," she said with a timid smile.

"You look so distraught," Mrs. Lincoln replied, gazing at her curiously. "What *is* it?"

Quickly, her voice trembling, Nettie told the President's wife about her younger brother, a Union soldier who had taken ill and was in a hospital in Alexandria.

"He needs personal care," she said. By now, she was crying again. "If he is not furloughed home, I feel certain he will die."

Mrs. Lincoln patted her shoulder. "Your brother shall have the furlough," she promised. "If Mr. Lincoln has to give it himself."

"Oh, thank you, thank you," Nettie said, sobbing.

Impulsively, she took hold of one of Mrs. Lincoln's tiny hands and kissed it. "God bless you, Mrs. Lincoln."

"There, there." The President's wife patted her arm, smiling. "Don't be concerned any longer."

Nettie drew in a deep, convulsive breath; the first breath of peace she'd drawn since word of her brother's presence in the Alexandria hospital had reached her.

"Well, then, that is settled," Mrs. Lincoln said. "Shall we begin?"

"Immediately," Mrs. Miller said.

She walked to the grand piano across the parlour and seated herself on its bench. Closing her eyes, she drew in deep breaths, seeking the rapid intercession of her Spirit guide.

Everyone stood silently, observing, as she continued breathing deeply, her expression one of intense concentration.

Several minutes later, her eyes jumped open and she quickly raised her hands, then brought them down sharply on the keyboard, the sudden loud sound making all of them twitch in surprise.

Mrs. Miller—or, as she would have it, her "control"—began to play a grand march.

The others stood and listened as the march was played with loud, resonant tones, Mrs. Miller's right foot pressing with intermittent force on the sustaining pedal.

Nettie felt herself becoming more tense by the moment, knowing what was coming. She felt her body tightening slowly, every muscle drawing taut, beyond her control.

When the music suddenly ceased, Mrs. Miller's hands jumping upward from the keyboard, the effect was as startling to Nettie as the start of her playing had been.

Without knowing why, the young woman's gaze jumped to the door.

It was opening.

She shivered at the appearance, in the doorway, of President Lincoln.

He's so *tall*! she thought, startled.

Wearing a dark blue suit made him appear even taller and seemed to accentuate the lined gauntness of his face.

Still, his warm smile overwhelmed all else as he closed the door and started toward them, moving with a slow, solemn pace.

"I heard the first notes of the march exactly as I reached the head of the grand staircase," he told them. "I kept step with it as I came down. It stopped precisely as I reached the parlour door."

As he drew near, Nettie could see, more clearly, how drawn his features were, how fatigued his movements.

He has so much responsibility, she thought.

She swallowed nervously as the President stopped in front of her; he seemed to loom overhead. She saw him raise his right hand—it's so *big*, she thought—then felt the gentle weight of it on top of her head.

"So," he said, smiling down at her. "This is our little Nettie, is it, that we have heard so much about?"

Her smile was that of a school girl, shy and embarrassed. "Yes, sir," she murmured.

"Come here," he said. His hand was lifted from her head and she felt his long, powerful fingers close gently around her left arm. He led her to an ottoman in front of a chair and seated her.

"You've been crying," he said.

His wife repeated, to him, what Nettie had told her about her brother in the hospital in Alexandria.

The President nodded with a kind smile. "Indeed, he will be furloughed," he said.

Nettie's breath trembled and she felt tears start to run down her cheeks.

"Thank you, sir," she whispered, "*Thank* you."

The President seated himself in the chair facing her and Nettie heard the soft, groaning sound he made as his large frame settled on the cushion.

He reached out both his hands and she gave him hers. They disappeared inside the magnitude of his.

"You know, of course," he said, "that I cannot openly declare belief in what you do or I would surely be pronounced insane and probably incarcerated. I can scarcely risk that when the fate of our nation is in such peril."

She answered in a muted voice. "No, sir."

The President smiled. "Well, how do you do it?" he asked.

Quickly, Mr. Laurie and Mr. Newton brought four chairs from across the room, arranging them to form a small circle including the President's chair.

Lowering the oil light, then seating everyone, Mrs. Miller to the President's left and Mrs. Lincoln to his right, Mr. Laurie next to his daughter, Mr. Newton next to Mrs. Lincoln, they all joined hands, the President releasing Nettie's hands and taking hold of his wife's hand with his right, Mrs. Miller's with his left.

Nettie sat encircled by the group.

She closed her eyes and drew in deep breaths, relieved that she no longer had to look into the deep, searching eyes of the President, knowing that she could never go into trance if she had to continue looking into those eyes.

Sounds began to intensify in her hearing. The crackling of the fire across the parlour; it seemed to be farther away with each passing moment. The occasional rustle of Mrs. Lincoln's skirt as she shifted on her chair. Once a soft clearing of his throat by the President.

At last, she felt the tickle of a spider web across her face and brow and knew that she was passing under control. Gratefully, she let it happen. She had been frightened that nothing would happen, humiliating her before the President.

Now, feeling the delicate webbing form across her features, she sank into the darkness with a peaceful sigh, allowing Dr. Bamford to come through.

❋   ❋   ❋

Her eyes jumped open and she looked directly into Lincoln's eyes.

No longer was her expression or voice those of an embarrassed schoolgirl. Now they were strong and forceful as she spoke to him.

"After the disaster at Fredericksburg," she said, Dr. Bamford said, "it is essential that you bolster the sagging morale of the Army."

The President watched intently as she continued. "Go in person to the front," she told him, "taking with you, your wife and children, leaving behind your official dignity and all manner of display."

"Resist the importunities of officials to accompany you and take only such attendants as may be absolutely necessary.

"Avoid the high grade officers to tents of the private soldiers. Inquire into their grievances. Show yourself to be what you are— the Father of your people.

"Make them feel that you are not unmindful of the many trials which beset them in their march through the dismal swamps, whereby both their courage and their numbers have been depleted."

She fell silent and the President cleared his throat to answer. "If that will do any good," he said, "it is easily done."

The voice of Dr. Bamford instantly replied. "It will do all that is required. It will unite the soldiers as one man. It will unite them to you in bands of steel."

"And now, if you would prevent a serious if not fatal disaster to your cause, let the news be promulgated at once and disseminated throughout the camp of the Army of the Potomac. Have it scattered broadcast that you are on the eve of visiting the front.

"Not that you are merely *talking* of it but that it is settled, that you are *going* and are now getting into readiness.

"This will stop insubordination and hold the soldiers in check, being something to divert their minds and they will wait to see what your coming portends."

"It shall be done," the President said.

Everyone started as Nettie Colburn stood. Looking down directly into Lincoln's eyes, she spoke to him with the utmost force and solemnity.

"You must not abate the terms of the issue uppermost in your mind," she declared.

The President's features tightened, the directive was so unexpected. He stared at the young woman's face as though it were the face of someone else.

"You must not delay its enforcement as a law beyond the opening of the year," Nettie told him. "This act will be the crowning event of your administration and your life."

The President twitched as Nettie placed her right hand on his shoulder. "You are being counseled by strong parties to defer the enforcement of it," she continued, her voice sounding too deep and resonant to be emerging from such a young, female throat. "These parties hope to supplant it by other measures and to delay action. You must, in no wise, heed such counsel but stand firm in your convictions, fearlessly perform the work and fulfill the mission for which you have been raised up by an overruling Providence."

Nettie Colburn fell silent then. Everyone stared at her expectantly.

Several moments later, she blinked and, seeing where she was, standing in front of the President, she started and, blushing, retreated so abruptly that she would have fallen back across the ottoman had Mr. Laurie not grabbed her suddenly by the arm.

The President stood, making Nettie cringe as he towered above her. Once more taking her small hands in his, he said, "My child, you possess a very singular gift. I thank you for coming here tonight. It is more important than perhaps anyone present can understand."

"Thank you, sir," she replied, feeling ill-at-ease.

While Mrs. Lincoln was thanking her profusely, Nettie was able to hear what Mr. Newton was saying to the President even though he spoke in a confidential tone of voice.

"Mr. President," he asked, "would it be improper for me to inquire whether there has been any pressure brought to bear upon you to delay the enforcement of the proclamation?"

"It is taking all my nerve and strength to withstand such a pressure," Nettie heard the President answer.

As they were exiting the parlour, Mr. Newton said to Lincoln, "Did you notice, Mr. President, anything peculiar in the method of address when Miss Colburn was addressing you in trance?"

"Yes, and it is very singular," Lincoln replied.

As they spoke, both men were looking at a full-length portrait on the wall.

That of Daniel Webster who had died in 1852.

AFTERWARD

Both injunctions given to the President that night by the twenty-year old medium were followed.

Lincoln's visit to the front, rallying the weakened Army of the Potomac, was a turning point in the Civil War.

And, on January 1, 1863, President Lincoln formally issued the Emancipation Proclamation, hastening the end of slavery in America.

Had the mediumship of this slender young woman altered the course of American history?

CELEBRITIES

So great was the interest in Spiritualism in the middle and latter half of the nineteenth century that some outstanding mediums became internationally known figures.

⁂ ⁂ ⁂

One of these was Andrew Jackson Davis.

Born in 1826, Jackson became noted for his clairvoyant ability, at one time giving an accurate description, cellar to garret, of a distant house.

He heard voices which imparted medical and spiritual counsel.

He—apparently—transmitted an extended discourse by the celebrated Greek physician Galen.

His "dictations" from the other side lasted from forty minutes to four hours, often spoken in languages and displaying a Biblical and scientific knowledge he knew nothing about in his conscious state.

Fourteen months and one hundred and fifty seven sittings resulted in a 782-page book entitled *The Divine Revelation.*

The book included an enormous amount of material from half a dozen sciences including astronomy, geology and archaeology.

All this from an uneducated, nineteen-year-old boy.

⁂ ⁂ ⁂

Another famous medium of this period was a Universalist preacher named John Murray Spear who became well-known for his gift at spiritual healing.

On one occasion, directed (according to him) by the spirits of Swedenborg and Benjamin Franklin, he was "led" sixteen miles without knowing why, finally ending up at the house of a woman recently struck by lightning.

His presence gave her immediate relief.

In addition to his continued healing accomplishments, Spear also delivered public lectures while entranced.

✳　　✳　　✳

The Koons family of Ohio became famous briefly for the so-called Spirit Room which—under spiritual "advisement"—they constructed in their house.

The room was in a log cabin twelve by fourteen feet with a seven foot ceiling.

It was furnished with seating for twenty people in addition to two tables and a rack for such instruments as a bass drum, two fiddles, a guitar, a French horn, a triangle, and a tambourine.

Conducting public seances, the mediumship of the Koons produced "spirit" concerts as well as lengthy communications from the Other World.

Reports indicated that the instruments, playing by themselves, gyrated wildly above the heads of the spectators.

✻ ✻ ✻

The Davenport brothers became widely known when, at the ages of sixteen and fourteen, they appeared in a public séance during which hands and arms were materialized and floating instruments played by themselves—despite the fact that both boys were carefully bound with ropes.

These séances were repeated for many years.

Famous author Richard Burton (translator of the *Arabian Nights*) attended four of the Davenports' séances and reported seeing musical instruments fly and play and feeling a "dry, hot and rough" materialized hand pull at his moustache and pat his head.

✻ ✻ ✻

Arguably the greatest physical medium in the history of Spiritualism, however, was Scotch medium Daniel Douglas Home.

Home counted among his supporters Count Tolstoy, Napoleon III and the Empress Eugenie as well as many of the crowned heads of Europe.

Literary figures who sat with him included William Thackeray, Anthony Trollope, Elizabeth Barrett Browning and Alexander Dumas.

Of Home's work, the famous British physicist, Sir William Crookes, wrote: *The phenomena I am prepared to attest are so extraordinary and so directly oppose the most firmly rooted articles of scientific belief—amongst others, the ubiquity and invariable action of the force of gravitation—that, even now, on recalling the details of what I witnessed, there is an antagonism in my mind between reason which pronounces it to be scientifically impossible and the consciousness that my senses, both of touch and sight, are not lying witnesses.*

D. D. Home

February 22, 1867
London, England

The four men—Lord Adare, Charles Wynne, Mr. Saal and Mr. Hurt—stood around the grand piano, trying with all their strength to push it down.

The piano hovered several inches in the air.

"Push it down," said Daniel Home. He stood nearby, arms raised. He was thirty-four, a man of striking appearance, clean-shaven except for his mustache, his reddish-blonde hair, bushy and curly.

The four men pressed down on the piano.

To their astonishment, instead of lowering, the instrument began to rise.

"Try harder," Home told them. He smiled at Mr. and Mrs. Jencken who were watching from the sofa of their sitting room. They smiled in response, totally entranced by what they were witnessing.

The piano kept rising. The four men leaned their elbows on its ebony top and forced their weight downward. All in vain. The piano continued to rise and they were forced to pull back or be lifted with it, their boots thumping on the rug as they dropped free. Reaching up, they gripped the upper edges of the piano with their hands and continued their teeth-clenching effort to stop the levitation of the heavy instrument.

Moments later, the bottom of the piano was above their heads, its top mere inches from the ceiling.

Mr. and Mrs. Jencken laughed softly. Although the room was not brightly lit, several lamps cast soft illumination and the flickering light of the fire was clearly visible on the underside of the piano.

After several more seconds, Home lowered his arms and the piano sank to the floor, making no sound as it touched the rug.

All four men applauded softly as well as Mr. and Mrs. Jencken. "Extraordinary!" cried Mr. Hurt.

The beaming Home turned to his host. "Mr. Jencken, would you join me, please?" he asked.

Mr. Jencken rose and crossed to the young Scotsman.

"Watch," Home told him. "Very closely now."

Jencken stared at him as Home drew in a deep, shuddering breath and began to stretch himself upward. Jencken's expression became one of startled disbelief.

Home was growing taller.

Jencken's mouth slipped open as he listened to the faint, crack-

44

ling noises emanating from the Scotsman's body. He, himself, was six foot tall and, already, the top of Home's head was higher than his own.

Across the room, he heard his wife catch her breath and one of the men murmur, "Oh my God."

Before the incredulous gaze of his sitters, Daniel Home extended himself to a height of six foot six inches, his face tight and strained, his expression one of pain.

Jencken started as Lord Adare spoke quietly. "Daniel, will you show us how it is?" he asked.

Slowly, as though each movement agonized him, Home unbuttoned his coat to reveal a gap of six inches between the bottom of his waistcoat and the waistband of his trousers.

Jencken looked more closely at the Scotsman. Unless his eyes deceived him, Home had grown in breadth as well, appearing, now, a veritable giant.

Abruptly, Home released a hissing breath and Jencken watched in awe as the young man slowly decreased in size. In less than two minutes, he had regained his normal height and breadth.

Home wavered then. Jencken felt himself twitch in surprise as Lord Adare stepped quickly from the shadows and grabbed the Scotsman's right arm, leading him to a chair.

"This is a feat which drains him terribly," he explained, seating Home in the chair.

Home sat with his eyes closed, filling his lungs with air. The group watched in silence.

"He'll be all right soon," Lord Adare reassured them.

Six minutes passed. The others seated themselves and waited, not speaking, their attention fixed on the young Scotsman who sat with his head back, his eyes closed, breathing deeply, working to regain his strength.

At last, he opened his eyes with a smile and looked around at them.

"Well, then," he said.

Pushing to his feet, he walked to the hearth and removed the poker from its rack. Jabbing at the coals, he made them spark and flare, the red coals whitening.

He placed the poker back into its rack and kneeled before the now crackling fire. As they watched, he drew in a long, deep breath.

Then reached into the fire with his right hand.

Mrs. Jencken made a faint, involuntary sound of horror as he did.

Home's movement did not waver. With his hand, he lifted up a red-hot coal the size of an orange.

Mr. Saal mumbled, "*Oh.*"

Home carried the glowing coal around the room, showing it to the group. Each reacted similarly, wincing and drawing back from its radiant heat.

After all of them had looked at it, the Scotsman returned to the hearth and dropped the coal back onto the fire.

He moved around the group again, showing them the palm of his right hand.

It was not scorched or burned. No skin was red or blackened. The palm appeared completely normal.

"So," Home said.

Returning to the fire, he knelt before it and began to stir the embers into flame again.

This time he used his hands to do so, causing Mrs. Jencken to emit the sound of horror once again, now more loudly.

"He's quite all right," Lord Adare assured her softly.

Despite his words, Mr. Jencken gasped as Home bent forward and placed his face among the burning coals. "Oh, no," she whispered.

"Steady," Lord Adare told her.

She gaped at the Scotsman. He was moving his face in the glowing coals as though bathing his face in comfortable water.

After several moments, he straightened up and they could see that his face was unaffected.

Reaching into the fire, he picked up the same large coal he'd previously handled. He stood and returned to the group, raising the coal toward his lips to blow on it and make it glow more brightly.

Mrs. Jencken put a hand across her eyes, unable to watch.

"I want to see which of you will be the best subject," Home said. "Ah! Adare will be the easiest because he has been the most with Dan."

"Why does he say that?" Mrs. Jencken whispered to her husband.

"His *Control* is speaking, not Mr. Home himself," he whispered back.

He stood on impulse as Lord Adare approached the Scotsman. "Put it in mine," he said.

His wife caught her breath, lowering her hand to look at him in shock.

"No, no, touch it and see," Home told him, stepping over to his host.

Jencken reached out gingerly and touched the coal for an instant, hissing with pain. Immediately, he placed the finger tip into his mouth to wet it. In moments, he would have a large blister there.

"Now you," said Home, holding the coal to within four inches of Mr. Saal's hand. Mr. Saal pulled his hand back automatically.

"Now you," Home said to Mr. Hurt, holding the coal a similar distance from his hand.

Mr. Hurt reacted in the same way, flinching and withdrawing his hand quickly.

Home turned to Lord Adare who was standing by him now.

"If you are not afraid," he said, "hold out your hand."

Obediently, Adare extended his right hand, palm up.

Using his left hand, Home made two rapid passes over the extended hand, then placed the burning coal in Lord Adare's palm.

"Good lord," Adare murmured. He stared at the coal in awe. "It feels scarcely warm," he said.

Home chuckled and picked the coal off his friend's palm. Carrying it back to the hearth, he dropped it onto the fire.

They all began to speak at once but Home restrained them with a sudden gesture, telling them, "The spirits are arranging something special. Do not be afraid and, *on no account*, leave your places."

Moving quickly to the window, he unlocked and raised it all the way. Mrs. Jencken shivered as the cold night wind came blowing in, billowing the curtains.

Home walked out of the room. In the adjoining study, they heard him opening another window.

Several moments passed.

Then Mrs. Jencken gasped and her husband said, "*Oh, my,*" his tone almost childlike.

Home was outside the window of the sitting room.

Standing upright in the air, seventy feet above the street.

With a smile, he "walked" into the room, bending over slightly to pass through the open window. Re-closing the window, he dropped into a chair and laughed.

"If a policeman had been passing by, imagine his astonishment if he had looked up to see Dan turning round and round along the outside wall of the house," he said.

He nodded toward the group. "Thank you for not having moved," he said.

Lord Adare rose without a word and walked into the study.

To his amazement, the window there was raised scarcely a foot.

Returning to the sitting room, he told the group, then, looking at Home, asked, "How is that possible?"

Home jumped to his feet. "Come and see," he said. He raised one hand to stop the others. "Only Adare, if you please," he said.

Lord Adare accompanied the Scotsman to the study. It was dimly lit but the illumination from the sitting room and from the gas lamps in the street made everything completely visible.

"Hold still," Home said.

He started leaning backward. Lord Adare twitched, about to make a move to catch the Scotsman, then froze as he saw that Home was not falling.

In a moment, Home was lying on his back in the air, completely rigid.

As Adare watched, open-mouthed, Home floated out through the opening, head first. For several moments, his body hovered in the air outside. Abruptly, then it floated back in, still horizontal.

Home was raised up and assumed his footing on the floor. He smiled at Lord Adare, patting the shoulder of his still gaping friend.

"Shall we return to the others?" he said.

AFTERWARD

No valid charge of fraud was ever brought against Home.

Hundreds of lawyers, scientists, physicians and journalists attended his séances.

All were convinced that what they witnessed was genuine, defying any normal explanation.

He produced solid, materialized hands in bright lamp light.

He played accordions suspended from one hand by his thumb and middle finger with its keys at the lower end.

He produced innumerable phenomena which defied the law of gravity.

On one occasion, a beautiful white hand materialized by Home placed a garland of flowers on the head of Elizabeth Barrett Browning.

When he died at the age of fifty-three, the inscription on his headstone read: *To another discerning of Spirits*.

He never charged a penny for his séances.

GROWTH

In addition to producing mediums as celebrities, Spiritualism now become a more respectable phenomenon as well.

Serious inquiries into its validity were initiated in 1869 by the London Dialectical Society.

In 1870, the Phantasmological Society at Oxford and The Ghost Society at Cambridge were created.

In 1882, the formidable Society for Psychical Research was established.

❋ ❋ ❋

It is interesting to note two points about Spiritualism during this period.

One: it was the first religion to endow dignity on the North American Indian because so many so-called Spirit Guides identified themselves as Indians.

Two: psychical researchers received a serious—and sympathetic—hearing from many eminent scientists of the day.

They have not attained such a level of scientific respectability since.

❋ ❋ ❋

Towards the end of the century, after D. D. Home was gone, the field of psychic phenomena required a new physical medium.

Said medium—the last of her kind—appeared in the person of a stout Italian peasant woman born in 1854.

Eusapia Palladino

December 9, 1909
New York, N.Y.

She held onto Carrington's arm as they walked along the third floor of the Lincoln Square Arcade building. He was aware of her firm grip, of the subtly intimate way she pressed against his side.

She was, perhaps, unaware of doing it, this seeking to establish a male-female relationship between them once again.

Why did she always do that? Carrington wondered. Did she truly believe he would allow himself to be more lenient to her because of it? Surely, she knew, by now, that she was mistaken in that assumption.

The footfalls of the group made irregular clacking noises on the hard tile floor, especially the heels of Carrington's wife (how all the more presumptuous the medium was, clinging to his arm in the presence of his wife) and Mrs. Humphrey.

Less audible were the falling heels of Mr. Forbes, Dr. Humphrey, Mr. Evarts and Carrington himself.

They reached 328 now and, withdrawing his arm from Palladino's hold, Carrington took the key chain from his trouser pocket and unlocked the door.

Reaching in, he switched on the overhead light and the group entered the small office.

As he went in, Carrington recalled momentarily, his renting of the office; how the owner had been taken back by his request for a sworn statement that the office was an ordinary one, free of trap doors or any other unusual features.

A faint smile raised the ends of his lips as he remembered the expression on the man's face when he said, in absolute perplexity, "*Trap doors? In an office?*"

Carrington had not explained.

Quickly and efficiently, he checked the safeguards in the office: the windows sealed and connected to burglar alarms; the special bolts on the insides of the windows and the special bolt and lock on the inside of the door.

None had been touched, of course. He had not expected that they had. Still, these preparations had to be conducted each time.

Critics loved to pounce on any safeguard overlooked, any precaution taken.

The cabinet—seven feet high and three feet on each side—was built into a special partition away from the back wall. It was open on the side facing the office, two curtains hanging across the opening, each made of lightweight black crepe.

Inside the cabinet was a wooden table on top of which lay a flute, mandolin, a music box, a small bell and a tambourine.

Even though Carrington knew that not a soul had entered this office since the previous sitting three nights past—their ninth—he, nonetheless, picked up each instrument and checked it thoroughly.

He was a methodical man and knew that he could never afford to indulge himself in the least bit of carelessness in his preparations for these séances.

"Very well," he finally said, nodding at Palladino as he set down the tambourine.

While the two women stepped inside the cabinet with the Italian medium to inspect her clothing and make certain she had nothing suspicious hidden on her person, Carrington checked the lights above the three-foot by two-foot table around which they would sit during the séance.

There was a cluster of five globes, the first an unshaded sixteen-candle-power lamp, the second an unshaded four-candle-power lamp.

The third lamp was the same power as the second but was shaded with tissue paper. The fourth, of similar power, was shaded with a thickness of red tissue.

The fifth, also four-candle-power, was shaded with two red screens.

Carrington examined them all. They varied from full illumination to a light in which the eye could make out only hands and faces.

Palladino came out of the cabinet with the two women, smiling to herself.

The women—especially Mrs. Humphrey—seemed embarrassed and Carrington suspected that, during the examination, Palladino had made some off-color (perhaps even lewd) remark; his wife had told him that the Italian woman was prone to such remarks during examinations.

Carrington avoided Palladino's dark-eyed glance at him when she sat down on her chair.

"So," she said. "The *strega* sits again."

She enjoyed referring to herself as a witch.

Carrington regretted her attitude. It was not that he felt personally critical but it made legitimizing her abilities all the more difficult.

What was it Mrs. Finch had called her in that editorial? "A monster of erotic tendencies?" It was scarcely that bad, but Palladino's behavior *did* make his work more onerous than it had to be.

It was hardly surprising that Hodgson had, so quickly, accused her of fraud. But then Hodgson always had been a pompous, waspish fool.

Carrington switched off the overhead light and, in the full illumination of globe number one, the group took their places, Palladino's chair with its back to the cabinet, two feet from the curtain, Mrs. Humphrey to her right, Mr. Forbes to her left; her "controls."

Palladino pressed her left leg against Mr. Forbes' right leg, making a soft, sensual sound as she did.

Mrs. Carrington, sitting across the table from her, glanced at her husband.

He could only shrug a little. There was nothing he could do. If he said anything remotely captious, Palladino might explode with instant rage and refuse to sit; her temper was mercurial, an ever-present threat.

Everyone in the group rested their hands on the table, fingers touching.

It was nine-thirty p.m.

❈   ❈   ❈

Eusapia Palladino raised her hands above the table, Mr. Forbes and Mrs. Humphrey holding their legs tightly against the medium's.

The table moved.

"Raps, please," Mr. Evarts requested.

On the table top, three faint raps were heard as though in reply.

Carrington freed his right hand momentarily to switch on globe number two and switch off globe number one. The room was now slightly dimmed.

Immediately, the table began to rock.

It, then, rose several feet into the air, was held suspended for a few moments, then lowered back to the floor.

At 9:42 p.m., Carrington again released his right hand to switch on globe number three and switch off globe number two. There was slightly less illumination in the office now.

The left-hand curtain on the cabinet blew out, then fluttered back into place.

The movement was repeatd.

Carrington changed the lighting once more, reducing it to the dim, reddish illumination of globe number four.

Again, their eyes adjusted to the change in light; they could still see very clearly despite the dimness. Both the medium's hands were visible above the table, being held by her controls. Both her legs were pressed against theirs.

"I've been touched on the right arm," Dr. Humphrey said.

Three loud raps were heard on the surface of the table.

At 9:48 p.m., the left-hand curtain of the cabinet again blew out and settled back into place.

Mr. Forbes' dry swallow was clearly audible in the silence. "I have Eusapia's hand firmly in mine but there is a hand behind the curtain touching my arm," he said.

"I have good control of Eusapia's right hand and foot," Mrs. Humphrey added.

The curtains blew out over Mr. Forbes' head.

"A distinct human hand is coming out of the curtain and touching me on the shoulder," he said. "I am holding the medium's left hand tightly."

"And I am holding her right," Mrs. Humphrey said.

At 9:55 p.m., Mr. Forbes gasped.

"My coat was grabbed by a hand and I was pulled toward the curtain," he said.

"Yes, I saw him pulled," Mrs. Humphrey verified.

Mr. Forbes cried out as his cigar case appeared on the cabinet table. "The case was in my inside coat pocket," he said. "A hand took it out."

As they watched, the cigar case opened itself. There was one cigar inside. "There were *three*," Forbes said, startled.

He gasped as a cigar was suddenly thrust between his teeth. He spit it out.

Palladino's hands were both in plain sight, two feet distant from the cabinet table.

At 10:02 p.m., the mandolin came floating from the cabinet and rested on top of Palladino's head. The bell on the cabinet table was heard clattering to the floor.

At 10:04 p.m., the flute sailed slowly out of the cabinet and touched Mr. Forbes on the shoulder.

Mrs. Humphrey caught her breath. "I feel a finger touching my right ear," she told the group.

The tambourine floated from the cabinet, rose in the air, waved back and forth, then dropped into Mrs. Humphrey's lap, startling her.

She and Mrs. Forbes reported that Palladino's legs and hands were still under their control.

The music box began to play in the cabinet. The tambourine rose from Mrs. Humphrey's lap and floated back into the cabinet, shaking itself. It came out again and hovered above the medium's head. All of them flinched as it was struck sharply three times.

At 10:19 p.m., everyone at the table felt a strong breeze coming from the cabinet.

"A hand is pinching my fingers," said Forbes. "I feel the flesh."

Palladino's hands and legs and feet were all controlled.

Carrington switched on globe number five and switched off globe number four. The office was almost dark now.

Mrs. Humphrey's chair was dragged from the table, then returned.

Four loud raps were heard on the table top. The cabinet curtains blew out violently.

"*Something black just came out of the cabinet,*" Dr. Humphrey said.

His wife made a frightened sound.

"There is a *white face*," Mr. Evarts said nervously.

"We see it," Carrington told him quickly. The atmosphere was becoming too tense, he thought.

At 10:41 p.m., the small table came out of the cabinet and appeared to climb onto the larger table, what looked like a hand grasping the small table.

The small table worked its way over to the edge of the séance table and fell to the floor beside Mr. Forbes, landing upside down. Both controls continued holding tightly to the medium.

At 10:44 p.m., a strong wind began to sweep around the room, chilling everyone. The curtains of the cabinet bulged out.

Mrs. Humphrey made a nervous sound. "Easy," Carrington told her.

Mrs. Carrington gasped in shock, looking toward the top of the cabinet curtains. The others followed suit and Mrs. Humphrey could not restrain a sob of dread.

A ghastly looking hand was floating near the ceiling, attached to part of an arm.

Mrs. Humphrey sobbed again as the hand floated down and settled on her husband's shoulder. "*Easy*," Carrington warned.

Suddenly, it vanished.

Mrs. Carrington cried out.

Hovering near the top of the curtains was a hideous, black, masklike form.

"*Remain still*," Carrington ordered.

Too late. Mrs. Humphrey went limp and started to slump forward in a faint. Tearing loose his hands, her husband moved to support her. Carrington could not control a sound of disappointment.

It was over.

The lights were turned up and Palladino helped to a chair by the window which was opened to give her air. Once more, Carrington was stricken by the change in her appearance. When they'd entered the office, she had been filled with energy, her black eyes alight with an almost diabolical mischief.

Now, after something more than an hour of sitting, she looked weak and drawn, nauseated, her face deeply lined. Amazingly, by tomorrow, after a night's sleep, her vitality and magnetism would be completely restored.

Forbes moved to the cabinet table. His cigar case still lay on top of it. He opened it and looked inside. There were three cigars again. Grimacing, he closed the case and noticed that the silver monogram which had been on the outside of the case had been violently torn off.

It would not be found in the office or ever seen again.

AFTERWARD

It was often claimed that Palladino was caught cheating.

That, when her hands were held by sitters, she was able to free one of them with spasmodic jerking movements until both sitters were holding part of the same hand.

This trick seemed to be confirmed by the fact that Palladino objected to having both hands held by the same sitter.

She also refused to be bound in any way.

On occasion, she even refused to let her legs be held.

Yet, it has been declared as too far-fetched that intelligent sitters, well versed in the tricks of mediums, almost always clinging with arms and legs to this elderly Italian woman, could be permanently fooled by foot and hand substitutions.

Her investigators were well aware of her duplicity.

Nonetheless, Sir Oliver Lodge—a world-renowned physicist and one of the most astute of psychic investigators—had this to say about Eusapia Palladino.

"There is no further room in my mind for doubt."

※　※　※

Palladino, herself, admitted that, upon occasion, she committed fraud.

"And always for the same reason," she stated. "You see, it is like this. Some people are at the table who expect tricks. In fact, they want them.

"I am in a trance. Nothing happens. They get impatient. They think of the tricks, nothing but tricks. They put their mind on the tricks and I respond.

"But it is not often."

※　※　※

The worst sitting Palladino ever gave was at Cambridge in 1895.

Psychic researcher Hereward Carrington claimed that this sitting was foredoomed because of the hostile presence of Dr. Richard Hodgson.

He stated that Palladino was actually encouraged to commit fraud.

That she was given every possible opportunity to do anything she pleased.

Hodgson even allowed her left hand to be free.

That Palladino availed herself of this opportunity was no surprise to Carrington.

Palladino was a simple woman, Carrington believed. Her ego compelled her to provide successful sittings.

Failure was unthinkable to her.

This streak of vanity was her undoing at Cambridge.

Still, to attribute all she did for more than eighteen years to a few simple, clumsy tricks is an insult to the intelligence and good sense of her many investigators.

To discount her phenomena, it must be stated categorically that every witness to it was either a fool or a liar.

Clearly, this was not the case.

BODY TO MIND

In the latter part of the nineteenth century, the emphasis on so-called "physical" mediums like Home and Palladino began to diminish to be replaced by a study of what came to be known as "mental" mediums.

Psychic investigators turned, with some relief, to this less taxing study of mediumship.

Now, the psychic, rather than performing feats of sound and movement—which were difficult to monitor, provided little in the way of genuine enlightenment and were sometimes dangerous to their investigators—offered information which often could not be verified and/or compared with established facts.

Two of the greatest of this new variety of psychic were Mrs. Leonore Evalina Simonds Piper (customarily referred to, simply, as "Mrs. Piper") of Boston and Mrs. Gladys Osborne Leonard (known as "the British Mrs. Piper") whose unusual careers were, in a number of ways, parallel to each other from children on.

Mrs. Piper and Mrs. Leonard

1867-1915

America and England

Returning home from school that day, Leonore went out into the garden to play.

It was a warm Spring afternoon in New Hampshire and the eight-year-old girl did not care to remain in the house.

For a while, she gathered acorns, crawling around busily to pick them up and place them in a small pail.

Then she sat on her favorite bench and methodically pushed them, one by one, through a hole in the wood which she had created by pressing down hard on a loose knot until it fell from the bench and landed on the ground.

She was so completely absorbed in her game that the blow caught her by surprise.

It was as though some invisible hand had struck her sharply on the right side of the head, over her ear.

She jerked erect with a gasp of startled pain, clutching at her head.

Inside the ear, she heard a hissing sound.

As she sat rooted to the bench, eyes wide with dread, the sibilant noise became a letter S being spoken by a woman's voice.

Then the voice said, *"Aunt Sara, not dead, but with you still."*

Leonore cried out, horror-stricken, and, bolting from the bench, ran into the house to her mother.

For several minutes, she was unable to speak a word, she was crying so hard and helplessly.

Then, between racking sobs, she managed to stammer, "Something hit me on the ear and Aunt Sara said she wasn't dead but with me still!"

Several days later, word was received from a distant part of the country that, at the very moment of Leonore's experience, her Aunt Sara had expired suddenly and unexpectedly.

※ ※ ※

Gladys Osborne showed equal evidence of being psychic at an early age.

It is not reported whether Leonore Simonds got in trouble for saying what she had but Gladys Osborne certainly did.

Because her father was leaving for Scotland that morning, eight-year-old Gladys was taken from her bed, clad in a dressing gown and brought downstairs to the dining room to have breakfast with him.

Scarcely awake, she sat in dutiful silence while he lectured her, telling her how he expected her to behave in his absence.

Too sleepy to concentrate on his words, Gladys stared at the wall across from her, enjoying the vision she had seen for several years now.

Before her lay a green valley bordered by verdant hills. The sky above was a sparkling blue, the light a vivid golden hue although there was no sunshine and no shadows.

Walking on the velvet-like grass, past banks of multi-colored flowers, were couples and groups of people dressed in graceful, flowing robes of varying hues. They all looked happy and contented.

As they always did.

"*Gladys*," said her father firmly.

She blinked and turned her head to look at him.

He was gazing at her with a frown of disapproval.

"What the devil are you looking at?" he asked.

She stared at him, not knowing what to say.

"You haven't heard a word I've spoken," he told her. "You've been staring at that wall the entire time. *Why?*"

She swallowed. "I...."

"*What?*" he interrupted. "What were you looking at? That pair of mounted pistols?"

"*Oh, no*," she said, concerned that he would think that.

"What then?"

She felt a sense of confusion. Dada didn't *see* it?

"My...place," she said. "My Happy Valley."

He gaped at her. "Happy—?" he began, then did not complete the phrase.

After several moments of dark appraisal, he did complete it. "*Happy Valley?*" he enunciated slowly.

"Yes, Dada."

William Jocelyn Osborne put down his cup of coffee and leaned across the table to peer suspiciously at his daughter.

"*What in the name of God are you talking about?*" he demanded.

※　※　※

At first, her father, then her family, thought that Gladys was making it up.

But when she persisted, describing, in such minute detail, what she saw, they became alarmed, then punitive.

Their orthodox beliefs did not include probing into "things which were not meant to be understood."

Gladys was forbidden to ever see this "Happy Valley" again.

In time, the visions—doubtless weakened by the collective negativism of her family, her doctors and friends—disappeared, leaving Gladys with a sense of deprivation.

❈ ❈ ❈

When Leonore Simonds was twenty-two, she married William Piper of Boston.

At the urging of her father-in-law—because she was suffering from the effects of an accident experienced some years earlier—Leonore was persuaded to consult a blind clairvoyant named J.R. Cocke who was attracting considerable attention by his uncanny medical diagnosis and subsequent cures.

Those who attended the meeting that Sunday night were seated in a circle around which the clairvoyant slowly moved, placing his hands on the head of each person in turn.

While he was standing opposite Mrs. Piper, diagnosing the afflictions of the woman seated across from her—on whose head Dr. Cocke's hands were resting—the face of the clairvoyant seemed to get smaller and smaller to her eyes as though it were receding into the distance.

Mrs. Piper began to lose all consciousness of her surroundings.

It did not return until the blind clairvoyant stopped behind her and placed his hands on her head.

Abruptly, she shuddered as a chill ran through her body.

She saw, in front of her, a flood of light in which a number of odd faces were hovering.

Then a hand passed to and fro before her eyes.

Dr. Cocke jerked his hands from her head as Mrs. Piper stood and walked around him to a table in the center of the room on which writing materials had been placed earlier.

Picking up a pencil, she leaned over and, for almost a minute, wrote rapidly on a piece of paper.

Then she turned, handed the piece of paper to an elderly man seated in the circle and took her chair again.

A few moments later, she started, re-focusing her eyes. Looking at her husband, she murmured, curiously, "What's happening?"

Everyone in the circle, except for the elderly man, stared at her in silence.

He was reading the piece of paper she had handed to him.

After a while, he looked up, an expression of awe on his face.

Rising, he moved to her and took both her hands in his.

"Young woman, I have been a Spiritualist for over thirty years," he told her, "but the message you have just given me is the most remarkable I have ever received. It gives me fresh courage to go on, for I know that my boy lives."

The man was Judge Frost of Cambridge, a noted jurist who had, for years, been seeking comfort for the loss of his only son.

The message Mrs. Piper had dashed off, unaware that she was doing so, was so filled with details only the Judge knew about that he was convinced of its authenticity.

In this manner, Mrs. Piper's psychic power was discovered.

※　※　※

When Gladys Osborne was twenty-four, she married Frederick Leonard, an actor.

One winter, during a poor engagement with a theatrical company that was visiting suburban theatres, she shared a dressing room with two sisters interested in Spiritualism.

The three of them had sat around a small table twenty-six times now, an hour every day between the matinee and evening performance.

Nothing whatsoever had happened.

One of the sisters, Nellie, became disheartened during their twenty-seventh sitting and decided to give it up. "Nothing's going to happen," she said. "There's nothing to it. Tables don't move unless somebody moves them."

Leaving the table, she sat at the other end of the room with a book and started to read.

Florence and Gladys remained at the table.

Two minutes later, it began to tilt up and down.

"Oh, my," said Nellie, returning quickly. She did not attempt to seat herself at the table, believing that her negative influence had prevented it from moving.

Instead, she picked up a pad and pencil and waited while Florence addressed whatever force she assumed was moving the table, asking it to tilt once for the letter A, two of the letter B and so on.

"My name is Feda." Nellie spoke aloud the first message after it had come through. "I am an ancestress of Gladys. I have been watching over her since she was born, waiting for her to develop her psychic power so I can put her into a trance and give messages through her."

Gladys and the two sisters stared at each other in wordless amazement.

It was the beginning of Mrs. Leonard's six decades of mediumship.

❈   ❈   ❈

A typical sitting (one of hundreds) by Mrs. Piper went as follows:

Sitting on an armchair in front of a table on which three pillows are placed, she carries on a casual conversation with the sitters.

More or less consciously, she slows her breathing and begins to look sleepy, her eyes becoming fixed and staring.

Soon the eyes become rigid, the breathing slows even more and, within five or six minutes, her head falls forward on a pillow, her pulse rate and breathing dropped well below normal.

Soon she sits up and her spirit control—at one point a so-called French physician named Dr. Phiniut—takes over the sitting.

❈   ❈   ❈

"I get the name Sarah," Dr. Phiniut says.

The sitter does not recall the name.

"Is there something wrong with your mother's foot?" asks Phiniut.

The sitter recalls some dropsical trouble her mother has with her foot.

Later, she remembers an aunt named Sarah.

Dr. Phiniut tells another sitter that "Agnes" will be ill that year. The month is March.

In the fall, Agnes becomes ill for the first time since childhood, spending a week in bed.

Phiniut also predicts the death of the sitter's uncle who is, at that time, in good health as far as the sitter knows.

Two weeks later, the uncle dies.

A Mrs. Pitman is told by Dr. Phiniut that she will have stomach trouble in Paris and it will be taken care of by a "sandy-complex-ioned" gentleman.

A short time later, Mrs. Pitman, traveling in Paris, is taken ill with stomach trouble and attended by a sandy-haired doctor.

"You will leave your home soon and settle in the city in a corner house," Dr. Phiniut tells a Mrs. M.E.C.

This presently comes true.

Phiniut addresses one of the sitters with a nickname unknown to anyone present.

Later, the widow of the deceased man (who supposedly spoke through Phiniut) reveals that the nickname was used by her husband's mother and sisters.

Phiniut tells a Mr. Perkins that his father believes he has heart trouble though he really hasn't.

Later, the father admits this, telling his son that he had not revealed this fear, even to his doctor.

The Thaws (in whose house the sitting is taking place) are told that W. was coming to them soon and that his kidneys are out of order.

This condition is not suspected at the time but is discovered two months later after W. shows up at their house.

"Your mother tells you again to put the thing you have on your lap around your neck," Dr. Phiniut instructs Miss Heffern.

Miss Heffern has always supposed the object—which is wrapped in paper—to be a lock of her mother's hair.

It turns out to be a religious necklace.

✳   ✳   ✳

Mrs. Leonard's most dramatic sitting came on December 3, 1915, in the house of Sir Oliver Lodge.

Approximately a week earlier Sir Oliver had received a letter from a B. P. Cheves mentioning a photograph taken of his son and a group of officers.

Lodge's son had been killed in France on September 14th.

At the séance, Lodge asked his son (through Mrs. Leonard's spirit contact Feda) if he recollected the photograph.

"Yes, there are several others taken with me," Raymond (through Feda) replied.

"Friends of yours?" asked Lodge.

"Some of them," Raymond answered. "They were not all friends."

"Are you standing in the photograph?" asks Lodge.

"No, sitting down. Some are standing and some are sitting."

"Were they soldiers?" asked Lodge.

"Yes, a mixed lot."

"Is it outdoors?"

"Yes, practically," Raymond answers.

Lodge is perplexed. "It must have been out of doors or not of doors. Do you mean *yes*?"

Mrs. Leonard (via Raymond and Feda) says it looks like a black background with lines going down.

She keeps drawing vertical lines in the air.

※　　※　　※

The photograph had been taken twenty-one days before Raymond's death.

He never mentioned it in his letters.

Raymond, in the sitting, is explicit about the following points:

1. His walking stick is visible.

2. There are considerable number of men in the photograph, the front row sitting.

3. A B. is prominent in the photograph. Also a C.

4. He is sitting down, the man behind him with his arm on Raymond's shoulder.

5. The background is dark with vertical lines.

When the photograph arrived, the following items were on it:

1. Raymond's walking stick is visible.

2. There are twenty-one men, the front row sitting on the ground. They are a "mixed lot" in that they are members of different companies.

3. Captain S. T. *Boast* is prominent. Also several officers whose last names begin with *C.*

4. Raymond is sitting, the officer behind him resting his hand on Raymond's shoulder.

5. The background is dark—with six, conspicuous vertical lines on the roof of the shed in front of which the officers are gathered.

Sir Oliver Lodge summed up the incident as follows:

The amount of coincidence between the description and the actual photograph surely is quite beyond chance or guesswork. Not only are many things right but practically nothing is wrong.

AFTERWARD

Of the two mediums, Mrs. Piper was probably the more outstanding.

Surely, she suffered more with her mediumship.

To begin with, her childhood was a dreadful one what with hearing voices, seeing faces and suffering with her bed rocking back and forth.

Although Mrs. Leonard was quoted as saying, "My childhood to me was a time of pain and torture," it seems evident that Mrs. Piper's childhood—and life—were more traumatic.

Certainly no medium in the history of Spiritualism was ever—willingly—so harshly treated by investigators.

Her nostrils tickled by a feather while she was in trance.

Her entire body pinched.

Lighted matches held to her arms.

Needles plunged into her hands while she in trance.

Pain pressure applied to her palms to a weight of twenty-five pounds.

A harsh price to pay for William James' opprobrium that Mrs. Piper was the one "white crow" disproving the "law" that all crows (mediums) are black.

※　※　※

Two of the more noteworthy aspects of the mediumship of Mrs. Leonard and Mrs. Piper were Mrs. Leonard's "book tests" and Mrs. Piper's "cross-correspondence."

One of Mrs. Leonard's "tests" came about after the Reverend

C. Drayton Thomas heard knocking sounds in his bedroom which he took to be spirit knocks.

At his next sitting with Mrs. Leonard he asked Feda if this was true.

Mrs. Leonard had never been in the Reverend's house but Feda's reply came as follows:

"You will be amused by the following test. There is a book behind your study door, the second shelf from the floor and fifth book from the left end.

"Near the top of page 17 you will see words which serve to indicate what Feda was attempting to do when knocking in your room."

Thomas located the book, a volume of Shakespeare. Near the top of page 17 was a line from *King Henry VI,* Act I, Scene 3.

"I will not answer thee with words but blows."

※　　※　　※

Between November 10, 1906, and June 2, 1907, Mrs. Piper gave 94 sittings during which 120 experiments in cross-correspondence were made.

These ran to allusions from classical literature and were like parts of a jig-saw puzzle being fitted together at a distance from each other.

A typical one follows:

The sitters—all educated men of great social respect—drew up a message in Latin so that Mrs. Piper could not possibly understand it. The message was directed to a similar group of deceased investigators.

We are aware of the scheme of cross-correspondence which you are transmitting through various mediums and we hope that you will go on with them.

Try to give to A and B two different messages between which no connection is discernible.

Then, as soon as possible, give to C a third message which will reveal the hidden connection.

Mrs. Piper was A.

This experiment extended from December 17, 1906, to June 2, 1907.

The dictation of the first sentence of the message (in Latin) took place over four meetings.

The second part of the message—sent to a different medium— came through by the middle of February, again in Latin.

By June 2, the entire message had been transmitted through Mrs. Piper and to the other two mediums, all in Latin which none of them understood.

The message turned out to be an elaborate poem by Robert Browning.

�֎   ✖   ✖

Both Mrs. Piper and Mrs. Leonard retired from mediumship at relatively early ages.

Ironically both lived far beyond the period of their greatest achievements.

Mrs. Piper died in 1950.

Mrs. Leonard in 1967.

FRAUDS

It is appropriate, at this point, to bring up the subject of fraud in mediumship.

While the accounts of genuine psychics have their interest, it would be unbalanced to not take into consideration the opposite aspects of parapsychology's beginning; that they were marked by— if not riddled by—dishonesty and outright swindling.

Of the Fox sisters, Houdini had the following to say. "They used Spiritualism as a means to 'get while the getting was good.'

Fortunately for the general public, Spiritualism received a severe jolt in the confession of Margaret Fox."

Of D. D. Home, Houdini said, "His active career, his various escapades and the direct cause of his death indicate that he lived the life of a hypocrite of the deepest dye."

Of Palladino, he said, "In her crafty prime, she may have possessed the agility and abundant skill in misdirection, together with sufficient energy and nerve, to bamboozle her scientific and otherwise astute observers."

Of the Davenport brothers, Houdini claimed to be an intimate friend of Ira Davenport who, he said, revealed to him that the brothers had practiced fraud and trickery throughout their careers.

And even told Houdini how their rope trick worked.

Describing Mrs. Piper's so-called spirit guide Dr. Phiniut, C.E.M. Hansel wrote: "He was adept at fishing for information and often contradicted himself. Also, he often displayed signs of temporary deafness when posed with a difficult question. Much of his 'communication' was garbled, incomplete or merely gibberish."

Describing Mrs. Leonard, Hansel wrote: "Her pronouncements were seldom impressive to anyone without a belief in Spiritualism," and that "When asked why she had remained so long with the Society for Psychical Research, she replied, 'Because of my desire to learn if I were possessed or obsessed.'"

The field of psychic mediumship is crowded with examples of fraudulent behavior in the séance room.

❋   ❋   ❋

A male medium, holding a sealed envelope, rubs a palmed sponge—soaked in odorless wood alcohol—over it which makes the envelope temporarily transparent, revealing the question on the sheet inside: *What about Uncle Shelby's will?*

The psychic clears his throat, declaring in sepulchral tones, "Your Uncle Sheldon—no, Shelby—sends his love and says—yes,

yes—seek out the Kingdom of the Lord, not gain from mortal legacy. Does that make sense to you?"

"*Oh, yes,*" the sitter answers.

✻ ✻ ✻

A sitter hands a female medium a multi-folded slip of paper— one inch by two inches—which the female medium slips into an envelope. She seals the envelope and holds it up so the sitter can see the folded note inside the thin envelope. She then proceeds to burn it all to an ash; leans over; concentrating on the ashes.

"This message comes from your...father, yes, your father. *Believe,* he says. Be thou a believer. Not like me. You understand this?"

"*Oh, yes,*" the sitter answers.

The explanation: the sitter hands the folded slip of paper to the medium. There is already a similar folded piece inside the envelope, glued in place opposite a two-inch slit in the envelope, then removed and palmed by the medium as she 'shows' the note to the sitter. Then she burns the envelope. The palmed note reads *Am I a skeptic like my father?*

✻ ✻ ✻

A darkened séance room. The male medium's voice is heard declaring gravely, "I feel cold water, surges of cold water and the splash and roar of angry sea." He sits beneath a large black hood, using a pen-size flashlight to read the message in a sealed envelope. *Brother Harry, did you suffer much when you were washed overboard and drowned?*

"I see a storm raging on the ocean now," the medium goes on. "I get the influence of a man—a blood relation—a father, no, a brother, a brother. He speaks his name. Ha...Ha...Harry. Do you understand?"

"Oh, yes," the sitter answers. Sobbing.

Later, the medium replaces the hood and flashlight under his shirt and his associate turns on the lights. The medium is still "in trance."

"As you can see," the associate says, returning the envelope. "It is still completely sealed."

"Oh, yes," the sitter says.

"Even if it weren't," says the associate, "who could read it in the dark?"

"Oh, yes," the sitter says.

※　　※　　※

A male sitter and a female medium sit across a table from each other, the sitter sponging off the surfaces of six slates. The medium's associate, standing to the left of the sitter, takes each slate in his left hand as it is cleaned and stacks the slates on a corner of the table.

There is a mantel behind the associate and sitter. As the fourth slate is being cleaned by the sitter, the associate retrieves another slate from a hiding place on the mantel. As he takes the cleaned slate from the sitter with his left hand, he instantaneously switches the slates and adds the prepared one to the pile on the table, placing the cleaned slates in the mantel hiding place.

The medium then slips a rubber band around the pile of six slates. "You are certain, are you," she rejoins, "that you have thoroughly cleaned each slate both back and front?"

"Oh, yes," the sitter answers.

Later, the prepared slate is "come upon" and handed to the sitter. On it is the message: *I greet you from the Life Beyond—send you my devotion, Mother.*

"Praise the Lord!" the associate cries.

"Oh, yes!" the sitter answers.

Overjoyed.

❋ ❋ ❋

The sitter stares at a cabinet in front of which is a blank canvas on an easel, a light shining through it from behind. The illumination in the room is low. Organ music plays mysteriously.

Inside the cabinet, the male medium is using a tiny hole in the curtain to spray an atomizer on the back of the canvas.

A face begins appearing on the canvas, that of a little girl.

The sitter sobs.

"Hallelujah!" cries the medium's associate.

Sulphocyanide of potassium is used for red, ferranocyanide of potassium for blue and tannin for black, the chemicals remaining invisible until sprayed with a weak solution of tincture of iron.

"You recognize the face?" the medium's associate asks.

"*Oh, yes!*" the sitter answers.

Weeping.

※　※　※

In the darkness, a female medium takes hold of the hand of the sitter to her left with her left hand. With her right, she removes a weighted artificial hand from beneath her robe and bends its flexible fingers over the arm of the sitter to her right.

"We must all sit very still now," she declares.

She picks up the trumpet from the table and begins to swing it around, then puts it to her lips and hisses into it, then grunts, then moans, then finally murmurs, "*Hel-oooooo.*"

"Hello," the sitter responds.

"Do you believe?" the medium asks through the trumpet.

"*Oh, yes,*" the sitter answers.

※　※　※

The male medium's associate stands in front of the cabinet, addressing the sitters. The medium's hand slips out between the cabinet curtains, removing, from beneath the bottom of his associate's robe, a veritable carload of luminous silk forms, faces, hands, costumes and reaching rods.

"Be it understood," the associate vows, "Professor Oglethorpe has nothing in this cabinet with him save his spirit friends."

"Oh, yes," the sitters say.

※　※　※

A séance room in darkness, a cabinet, its curtains extending to the ceiling.

Inside, a trap door is raised in the ceiling, a padded ladder lowered. Down which descend an endless legion of spirits enacting their ethereal performances.

※　※　※

All of these mediumistic ploys were well known to Harry Houdini.

He used all of them to discredit what he believed to be fraudulent psychics.

Occasionally, he went too far.

Margery

August 19-20, 1924
Boston, Massachusetts

The dark hotel room was so still that even the shifting of his light weight on the chair was audible.

Houdini spoke suspiciously. "You have her hands grasped firmly?" he demanded.

Dr. Prince sighed. "I have her left hand held in mine," he answered.

Would the little man ever be satisfied? he wondered.

"I have the right hand," Dr. Crandon said slowly and distinctly. "As always."

"Yes, *her* husband," muttered Houdini.

"*You* accepted him, sir," Malcolm Bird reminded the magician.

Along with Dr. Comstock, Hereward Carrington and Professor MacDougall, he sat some distance from the cabinet.

Houdini made a disgruntled sound. His small hands swept

quickly above the surface of the table which separated him from the cabinet.

Then he touched the electric light wired to a telegraph key; the bell box.

Mina Crandon, known to the psychic world as Margery, sat in the heavy wooden cabinet, only her head and hands protruding. Her eyes were closed, her head slumped forward.

"Very well," Houdini addressed her. "Ring the bell if you can. Let me hear the bell ring."

The bell rang so immediately that his look of smug assurance vanished in an instant, replaced by one of angry surprise.

"Are you *satisfied?*" asked "Walter."

※　　※　　※

"Contrary to all the newspaper reports," Houdini told them before the next sitting, "I have *not* been baffled along with every other investigator."

"You're *still* not convinced?" Malcolm Bird looked offended. "You heard the bell last night. We all heard it."

"Obvious fraud," Houdini responded.

"Mr. Houdini." Bird's features tightened with resentment. "Every single condition in the séance room—down to the very construction of the solid wood cabinet—was yours."

"Completely false," the magician said. "The conditions were *not* mine.

"Further, I accuse you, Mr. Bird, of being totally untrustworthy and I forbid you from being present in the séance room any longer. I have canceled a valuable stage tour to attend these sittings and I will not be trifled with or lied to."

Malcolm Bird, infuriated, could barely speak. "That's it for me," he managed to say before he stormed from the room.

Houdini's smile was cold. "Perhaps now we can have an *honest* test," he said.

Fifteen minutes later, Mina Crandon, attired in dressing gown, silk stockings and slippers, was helped into the cabinet by her husband.

Houdini shut the cabinet and locked it carefully. "*Now,*" he said.

He looked at Dr. Crandon. "Professor MacDougall will hold your wife's right hand this evening."

"You don't trust me either?" Dr. Crandon challenged.

"In matters of this sort, I trust no one," Houdini answered. "Least of all, you, the subject's husband."

"You believe I will deliberately assist her in deceiving you," Dr. Crandon said, his expression one of ill-contained rage.

"I believe it possible that you already have," Houdini replied.

Dr. Crandon shuddered, attempting to repress his fury. "She is accustomed to my holding her right hand," he said.

A look of anger twisted the magician's face. "Either Professor MacDougall holds her right hand or I will declare this sitting null and void and consequently do all within my power to discredit any further sittings by your wife."

Dr. Prince took hold of Dr. Crandon's arm to restrain him. Crandon looked at him abruptly, then back at Houdini. He was about to speak when his wife said, "It's all right, Goddard. Let it be."

Dr. Crandon filled his lungs with slow, deep breath, then nodded once and moved to one of the chairs against the wall.

"Dr. Prince will, as usual, hold the mediums' left hand," Houdini said, giving the word 'medium' an emphasis of obvious scorn.

Dr. Crandon began to rise from his chair, then sank back down as Carrington reached out and gripped his shoulder.

"The man is intolerable," Crandon murmured.

Carrington's smile was partly sad, partly amused. "I know," he replied quietly.

As Dr. Comstock was moving to extinguish the lights, Houdini said, "One moment, I want to check the cabinet again."

"Dear God." Dr. Crandon looked around the room as though to avoid the sight of the small magician as Houdini unlocked and opened the cabinet again, then peered inside, feeling around the interior, aided by his assistant.

"Very well," he finally said.

He closed the cabinet again and re-locked it. He and his assistant took their places by the table as Dr. Comstock turned off the lights and felt his way to his chair.

Within a minute, Margery's "control"—ostensibly her deceased brother Walter—burst through, his voice incensed.

"We will not continue with this sitting!" he said. "The *magician* plans to trick us!"

"*What?*" Houdini sounded outraged.

"He has hidden a collapsible ruler under the cushion beneath the medium's feet!" raged "Walter." "There will be no sitting! Turn on the lights!"

A frowning Dr. Comstock rose and felt his way back to the light switch.

"I forbid this!" cried Houdini.

"*There will be no sitting!*" Walter cut him off.

As the lights went on, Houdini lunged to his feet and over to the cabinet, features stone-like. With quick, angry movements, he unlocked the cabinet and threw it open. Reaching down, he jerked a folded ruler from beneath the cushion under Mrs. Crandon's feet; held it up in triumph.

"Announcing the existence of this ruler is obviously a cheap device to avoid its discovery and, at the same time, discredit me," he said derisively.

"A cheap device to discredit my wife, you mean!" Crandon broke in loudly. Again, he had to be restrained by Carrington.

Houdini pointed at the cabinet, his expression one of contempt.

"I accuse our so-called *medium* of concealing this ruler in the cabinet to besmirch my reputation!" he cried.

"A lie!" raged Crandon.

"Mr. Houdini, you and your assistant checked the cabinet completely just before we started," Dr. Prince reminded him.

"We did not—" began Houdini.

"You even re-opened the cabinet to check it again mere seconds before we started," Prince interrupted the magician.

"In order to place the ruler inside and discredit my wife!" Dr. Crandon shouted.

"False!" Houdini screamed at him. "*False! False! False!*"

AFTERWARD

The mystery was never solved. Houdini denied that he had placed the ruler in the cabinet. So, too, did Dr. Crandon and his wife.

At the very least, Houdini's accusations of fraud in this case were questionable.

❋ ❋ ❋

Oddly enough, although it is generally assumed that Houdini went to his grave claiming that he had never witnessed a single, genuine psychic manifestation in his life, he once told Hereward Carrington that, while performing in Berlin, he had, in fact, experienced exactly such a manifestation.

He was walking onto the stage to begin his show when his eyes were drawn to the opposite wing.

There, he saw his mother standing, a shawl over her head.

Smiling at him.

Torn between his sense of duty to the audience and his stunned reaction to the sight of his beloved mother, Houdini spoke a few words of greeting to the audience, then looked back quickly at the wing where he had seen his mother.

She was gone.

Houdini, stricken, commenced his show.

Later, to discover that, at the moment he had seen his mother, she was dying in New York.

✳ ✳ ✳

Even more odd—if not downright peculiar—is the conviction that Houdini's declared vow to communicate with his wife after death never took place despite yearly attempts on his birthday.

In fact, he *did* communicate with his wife as agreed.

At least, his widow believed that he did.

✳ ✳ ✳

In a message delivered by well-known medium Arthur Ford—through his Spirit Control Fletcher—Mrs. Houdini was told the following:

"A man who says he is Harry Houdini but whose real name was Ehrich Weiss, is here and wishes to send to his wife, Beatrice

95

Houdini, the ten-word code which he agreed to do if it were possible for him to communicate.

"He says you are to take this message to her and, upon acceptance of it, he wishes her to follow out the plan they agreed upon before his passing. This is the code: "ROSABELLE**ANSWER**TELL**PRAY**ANSWER**LOOK** TELL**ANSWER**ANSWER**TELL""

No one on earth knew this code but Houdini and his wife.

※　※　※

Following another sitting with Arthur Ford, Mrs. Houdini stated emotionally, "It is right!"

The code was used by her and Houdini in their "mind-reading" act.

Interpreted, the message was ROSABELLE, BELIEVE.

※　※　※

Mrs. Houdini prepared a hand-written statement as follows:

Regardless of any statements made to the contrary, I wish to declare that the message, in its entirety, and in the agreed upon sequence given to me by Arthur Ford, is the correct message prearranged between Mr. Houdini and myself.

Beatrice Houdini

※　※　※

From the moment Mrs. Houdini signed this statement, she was exposed to a firestorm of scorn and criticism.

It is believed that she later reneged on her signed statement.

At least, virtually everyone believes that she did.

But the facts remain.

MEDIUM MOST RARE

The era of the great mediums was coming to a close.

Spiritualism was waning.

Psychical research was now concentrating on effects and general tests rather than on individual psychics.

Only one figure remained as the era neared its conclusion. The last truly rare medium.

Arguably, the most rare medium in the history of parapsychology.

Edgar Cayce

May 2, 1890
Hopkinsville, Kentucky

By the streamside, he had built a lean-to of saplings, fir branches, moss, bark and reeds.

He was sitting there that afternoon, reading the Bible.

He was only thirteen but he'd read it twelve times and his plan was to complete his thirteenth reading of it by the end of the year.

He was in the middle of a verse from Jeremiah when he sensed a presence.

Looking up, he saw a woman standing in front of him. The blinding sunlight behind her made it difficult for him to see her clearly.

He started as she spoke to him, her voice soft yet perfectly audible.

"Tell me what you would like most of all so that I may give it to you," she said.

The boy was awed and frightened even though the woman's voice had been benign.

He winced as he saw something moving behind her shoulders. Something like wings.

Edgar swallowed dryly, just managing to respond.

"Most of all, I'd like to be helpful to others," he said. "Especially to children when they're sick."

He blinked.

The woman was no longer there.

He sat rooted to the ground for several minutes, gaping at the spot where the woman had been standing.

Then, jumping to his feet, he ran all the way home to tell his mother.

She was in the kitchen making supper and he blurted out his story.

When he was finished, he asked her, "Do you think I've been reading the Bible too much? It makes some people go crazy, doesn't it?"

Mrs. Cayce smiled and put her arms around his.

"You're a good boy to want to help others," she told her son. "Why *shouldn't* your prayer be answered?"

※　※　※

Edgar hit the floor again and sprawled there, breathless.

His father, Squire Cayce, hauled him to his feet and set him down hard on the parlor chair.

Snatching the spelling book off the floor where it had landed when he'd cuffed his son, Squire Cayce slapped it onto Edgar's lap, making the boy wince.

"You will not disgrace the family," Squire Cayce told him sternly. "You will stay up all night if need be but you *will* learn to spell the words in that lesson. I will not have a stupid son."

He pointed at the cowering boy. "Now get to business," he commanded. "I'll be back again in another half hour."

He left the room and the groggy Edgar re-opened his spelling book. It had been a long evening for him. Every time his father had asked him to spell the words from his current lesson, Edgar had failed.

Sniffling, he leaned over the book and began to study again.

At half past ten, Squire Cayce strode into the room and grabbed the speller from his son's hands.

"Spell *capital*," he ordered.

"C-a-p-i-t-i-"

He cried out as his father, totally exasperated, smacked him on the left side of the head and sent him flying off the chair.

He pointed fiercely at his huddled son.

"I am going into the kitchen for a few minutes," he said ominously. "When I come back, I am going to ask you that lesson once more.

"It's your last chance."

He stormed out. Edgar, tired and sleepy, left ear ringing, sat up slowly, trying not to cry.

He froze as he heard a woman's voice; the voice he'd heard in the woods that day. "If you can sleep a little, we can help you," it said.

Edgar looked around dazedly. The room was empty.

He twitched as the voice repeated, "If you can sleep a little, we can help you."

Edgar groaned weakly. How could it get any worse no matter what he did? he thought.

Closing his spelling book, he put it on the floor and laid down with his head on top of it. In seconds, he had fallen sound asleep.

His father woke him up ten minutes later by yanking the speller out from under his head so that his skull thumped down on the floor.

"All right," his father said in a threatening voice. His tone made it obvious that he was sure that nothing had changed.

Grabbing Edgar by the left arm, he pulled him to his feet and sat him on the chair again. "*Capital*," he ordered.

"C-a-p-i-t-a-l," the boy replied.

The Squire's eyes narrowed suspiciously.

"*Household*," he said.

"H-o-u-s-e-h-o-l-d," the boy responded.

"*Valid*," said the Squire.

"V-a-l-i-d."

When Edgar had spelled every word in the lesson correctly, his father went on to the next lesson. The boy spelled every word in that lesson as well.

Then the boy said, "Ask me anything in the book."

The Squire's face was getting red now. Glaring from the book to Edgar and back again, he skipped through the speller at random, picking out the hardest words he could find—which Edgar spelled correctly.

When the boy said, "There's a picture of a silo on the next page, the word *synthesis* under it—s-y-n-t-h-e-s-i-s."

The Squire slammed the book down in a fury.

"What kind of nonsense is this?!" he roared. "You knew that lesson all the time! You knew the whole blessed book!"

"Yes, because the angel—" Edgar broke off with a cry of pain as his father whacked him on the head again, knocking him off the chair.

"Go to bed!" the Squire shouted. "Before I lose my temper!"

※　　※　　※

The headaches had been plaguing him for weeks now. By the time he reached Elkton, the pain had become severe and constant.

Edgar couldn't find the strength to sell anymore. Locating the nearest doctor, he visited the man's office and asked for a sedative.

The doctor gave him some powder in a folded square of paper and, as soon as he arrived at his hotel, Edgar poured the powder into several inches of tap water, stirred it with an index finger and swallowed it in one gulp. Then he lay down on the bed to try and sleep.

It was March, 1900.

When he opened his eyes again, two doctors were leaning over him, looking very grave.

"How do you feel?" one of them asked.

Edgar tried to answer but was unable to summon more than a whisper.

Shocked, he tried again; in vain. He looked at the doctors frightenedly.

Then he looked around, experiencing a jolt of new dismay.

He was no longer in the hotel room but in his bedroom at home.

He had no recollection whatever of being taken there.

✳   ✳   ✳

His voice had never returned.

In the ensuing year, Edgar, unable to speak above a painful whisper, had been forced to give up being a salesman and became, instead, a photographer's apprentice.

In an attempt to regain his voice, he had been working with a local hypnotist named Al Layne. But every time he'd reached a certain level of hypnosis, something had held him back.

Until the afternoon of March 31, 1901.

Edgar was in the parlor of his home, lying on a horsehair sofa, eyes shut. Sitting in a chair beside the sofa was Al Layne.

Across the room, Edgar's wife Gertrude was sitting with his parents, all observing worriedly.

After yet another attempt to get him to speak normally proved fruitless, Al Layne told them that he was going to try something different.

"Edgar," he said, "instead of trying to speak, *look inside your throat* and see if you can find out what the problem is.

"Take your time. Look carefully inside your throat and, when you're ready, tell us what you see. And tell us in a normal tone of voice."

Edgar Cayce remained motionless on the sofa, eyes closed. His wife and parents stared at him in concern.

Several minutes passed in silence.

Then Edgar began to speak to himself. They all leaned forward in their chairs, straining to hear, but could make no sense of what he was mumbling.

Finally, he cleared his throat.

"Yes," he said, "we have the body."

They all stared at him in mute astonishment as he continued, his tone so clear that it was difficult to believe that, moments earlier, it had been no better than a barely audible, rasping sound.

"In the normal state," said Edgar Cayce, twenty-three, "this body is unable to speak due to a partial paralysis of the inferior muscles of the vocal cords produced by nerve strain. This is a psychological condition producing a physical effect.

"This may be removed by increasing the circulation to the affected parts by suggestion while in this unconscious condition."

Al Layne's mouth hung open. It did not occur to him for close to a minute that he needed to respond to the young man.

Abruptly, then, he said, "The circulation to the affected parts will now increase and the condition will be removed."

Edgar reached up to unbutton his shirt. Al Layne started, then leaned forward quickly to open the shirt, baring the young man's chest.

He caught his breath.

The upper part of Edgar's chest was turning pink, the color slowly spreading upward to his neck.

"My God." Squire Cayce was on his feet now, staring at his son with an awestruck expression.

Now his wife stood up beside him, then Gertrude Cayce. With the hypnotist, they watched incredulously as the pinkness on Edgar's chest turned to a roselike color, then increased to a vivid, burning red, Gertrude and his mother wincing at the sight.

For twenty minutes, Edgar Cayce's wife and parents stood in silence, gaping at Edgar's neck and chest.

They twitched in surprise as the young man cleared his throat.

"It's all right now," he said, his voice still normal. "The condition is removed. Make the suggestion that the circulation return to normal and that, after that, the body awaken."

Layne swallowed dryly and did as he was told and they saw the fierce redness fade through rose and pink, back to normal flesh tone.

Edgar Cayce opened his eyes and sat up. Removing a handkerchief from his trouser pocket, he coughed into it and the four people saw a small amount of blood soak into the white cotton.

Then he looked at Al Layne. "*Hello*," he said.

A smile of overwhelming joy pulled back his lips. "I can talk!" he cried. "I'm all right!"

His wife and mother, weeping, ran to embrace and kiss him. Squire Cayce, speechless with emotion, moved to his son's side and grasped his hand.

Al Layne could only stare.

In all his years of working with hypnosis, he had never seen the like.

AFTERWARD

So began the healing life of Edgar Cayce, the most incredible psychic of our century.

For more than forty years, this simple Kentucky man, with no medical training whatsoever, or much education of any kind, diagnosed the nature of every patient's ailment—*many of them hundreds of miles distant*—and recommended treatment.

Edgar Cayce healed literally *thousands* of men, women and chil-

dren—of appendicitis—arthritis—tuberculosis—intestinal fever—
hypertension—hay fever—polio-diabetes—and hundreds of other
illnesses and injuries.

In all, Cayce gave 14,256 psychic readings yielding 145,135 tran-
script pages over a period of 43 years.

Not once did he contradict himself.

❊ ❊ ❊

In addition to his physical readings, Cayce also gave psychic
readings in which he discussed the history of Man on Earth.

Through these readings, he was able to predict accurately a
number of archaeological discoveries decades before they were
made, regarding not only known civilizations but lost civilizations
as well, the existence of which had not been uncovered when the
predictions were made.

Describing this pre-historic world, he spoke about the extreme
northern portions—the polar regions—as existing in the southern
portions—the tropical regions; the Nile emptying into the Atlantic;
the Sahara fertile and inhabited; the Mississippi Basin under miles
of ocean, the only visible area of what is now the United States
being portions of Nevada, Utah and Arizona.

The Atlantic Ocean, he claimed, was mostly the continent of
Atlantis.

The Pacific Ocean, he claimed, was mostly the continent of
Lemuria.

※   ※   ※

Regarding Cayce's amazing record of healings—especially those at great distances—it has been questioned as to whom he was referring when he used the word "we" while diagnosing and prescribing cures for illnesses.

Was it the so-called "editorial we"?

Or did "we," in fact, refer to the so-called "spirit doctors" who were ostensibly conferring with him?

This interpretation seems the most acceptable.

The alternative is that he utilized some incredibly complicated telepathic and/or clairvoyant hook-up to the brains of hundreds of living doctors and the—often remote—locations of hundreds of exotic balms and medications.

THE NEW APPROACH

Psychical research—now formally given the name of Parapsychology is, today, part of the curriculum at major colleges and universities.

Harvard. Yale. Columbia. Duke. Cambridge. Oxford.

While not given the extensive respect it received at the turn of the century, psychical research has, nonetheless, achieved a plateau of genuine acceptance by part of the scientific world.

Part of this acceptance is due to the laborious work of one man at Duke University: J. B. Rhine

For the first time in the history of psychical research, telepathy

109

was studied by serious investigators as the primary aspect of psychic ability.

This was a calculated extension of earlier tests which discovered that patients, in mesmeric trances, often responded to unspoken thoughts.

※   ※   ※

Tests were given by Janet and Gurney establishing the correct identification of pain by telepathy.

Often, when the hypnotist pinched himself (or herself) the subject "felt" the pain.

※   ※   ※

Experiments were conducted by Professor and Mrs. Henry Sidgwic in which two-digit numbers selected at random and "visualized" by the hypnotist, were transferred telepathically to entranced subjects in adjoining rooms.

A vital aspect of these experiments was the adoption of mathematical evaluation of the test results.

※   ※   ※

The introduction of statistical methods for evaluation became standardized, using playing cards as "targets."

※　※　※

Important test results were obtained with the use of a board divided into 48 squares.

※　※　※

Three series of telepathy tests were conducted, using the color and suit of playing cards exclusively.

A success ratio of more than eight million to one was achieved by these tests.

※　※　※

Tests were introduced to examine clairvoyance as a phenomenon differing from that of telepathy.

※　※　※

Special testing cards known as Zener cards were developed by Rhine.

Five simple shapes were utilized, one on each card, five cards with each symbol for a pack total of twenty-five.

Every known aspect of psychic ability was examined with the use of these cards.

✱ ✱ ✱

In 1934, Rhine's monograph entitled *Extra-Sensory Perception* first coined the term ESP and replaced the term "Psychical Research" with "Parapsychology."

✱ ✱ ✱

In 1933, and '34, Rhine initiated tests to study the phenomenon of precognition (the prediction of future events) and psychokinesis (the power of mind over matter).

✱ ✱ ✱

While none of this could, in any way, match the drama and/or flamboyance of the great nineteenth century mediums, it did endow the field with a definite aura of academic respectability.

✱ ✱ ✱

The difference between the era of mediumship and the establishment of parapsychological testing was a simple but profound one.

In the nineteenth century, special mediums were examined and tested.

In the twentieth century, with few exceptions, only so-called "ordinary" people were examined and tested.

It is now generally believed that everyone has some psychic ability.

The testing procedure inaugurated by J. B. Rhine and his wife indicated that one in five persons demonstrated these abilities.

Rhine was quoted as saying, "The most experienced investigators have come more and more to accept the view that, while individuals differ greatly in their potentialities, most people—probably all—possess some of these parapsychical abilities in some degree."

※   ※   ※

It is interesting to note that Dr. Rhine and his wife initially established all of their scientific procedures to investigate their major interest.

Survival after death.

CONCLUSION

Parapsychology today would interpret the incidents dramatized in this book in a far different way then they were interpreted when they first occurred.

※   ※   ※

The King Croesus incident, for example, appears to be an ancient precursor of what parapsychologists, today, call distance vision—or remote viewing—a form of "traveling" clairvoyance.

In this case, the clairvoyant ability of the sixth oracle allowed him to view and describe what the King of Lydia was doing at some distance, namely cooking a tortoise and a lamb in a brass cauldron.

※　※　※

Sister's Teresa's spontaneous rising into the air, on the other hand, would indicate a form of what today's psi investigators would likely refer to as levitation.

This is an area of study not well advanced in parapsychology in that it appears to indicate an ability to negate the law of gravity, a feat even today's more lenient parapsychologists would not be inclined to advocate in any way.

※　※　※

Swedenborg's ability to "see" his house on fire three hundred miles distant would, of course, again be suggestive of distance vision.

His ability to locate the hidden drawer in the desk of the deceased Dutch ambassador would probably be interpreted, by contemporary parapsychological thought, as an example of telepathy in that the ambassador's wife knew, if only sub-consciously, (via telepathy from her husband when he was alive) about the drawer's existence.

That the incident might illustrate, to any degree, the existence of communication from consciousness existing beyond the grave (life after death) not many of today's psi investigators would even consider much less entertain any concession of likelihood.

※ ※ ※

At any rate, all of these events are little more than anecdotal.

It is only with the advent of Mesmer's work that any degree of "scientific" application to psychic events is noted.

His consulting rooms might, in a general—admittedly crude—manner be considered as the first parapsychological testing laboratory.

The inducement, via "Mesmerism," of various psychic manifestations such as telepathy, clairvoyance and self-diagnosis could certainly be considered an initial step in psychical research.

Especially in light of the fact that it led directly to the acceptance of the phenomena which we still refer to as *hypnosis*, a major tool in the study of man's "inner" mind.

※ ※ ※

With the Fox sisters (a prime example of telekinesis?), the background of modern parapsychology becomes definite in outline.

By laying the ground work for the establishment of the Spiritualism movement, the main stepping stone to modern parapsychology was set in place.

As indicated, historians date the birth of Spiritualism at 1848, the year the Fox sisters first began to experience the odd events in Hydesville, New York.

✻ ✻ ✻

The incident with D.D. Home is an example of one of the greatest—if not *the* greatest—physical mediums in the history of Spiritualism in action.

Although very few of the phenomena displayed by the Scotch medium are, as yet, grist for the mill of today's parapsychologists, they represent—if literally true—an incredible display of inexplicable (to date) occurrences.

The apparent elongation of his body.

His ability to handle hot coals without injury.

His reported levitation through the window opening of Lord Adare's sitting room.

Admittedly more colorful than scientifically verifiable, these phenomena were certainly of great dramatic impact.

✻ ✻ ✻

The incident at the White House in which young Nettie Colburn gave so-called psychic advice to President Lincoln doubtless would be interpreted by today's parapsychologists as a prime example of telepathy in that Lincoln was only told what he had been giving much thought to and wanted very much to hear in his anxiety to make a decision regarding both a necessary visit to the Union troops and the formal issuance of the Emancipation Proclamation.

That the voice with which Nettie Colburn spoke was apparently that of Daniel Webster could be interpreted as signifying that Lincoln needed some truly strong presence to voice his own inner convictions and Daniel Webster was a perfect choice for that presence.

※　※　※

The sitting with Eusapia Palladino, while more prosaic than that of D.D. Home, is indicative of a new, closer examination of physical mediums in that period, an attempt to apply more stringent testing methods to the study of psychic phenomena; a new step forward in the gradual progression toward modern parapsychological procedures.

※　※　※

The remaining dramatizations—Mrs. Piper—Mrs. Leonard, Margery (with Houdini) and Edgar Cayce complete the step-by-step progression from the pre-history period of parapsychology to its present day existence.

✖   ✖   ✖

Despite the impressive advances made by parapsychologists all over the world, there still remains one unavoidable element of doubt in the scientific community.

How can psi contribute anything relevant to the mainstream of science since the tools of science cannot be utilized to study phenomena which are so elusive and unpredictable?

This criticism, of course, is not completely valid any longer.

Advances in instrumentation and experiment design have made the studies of parapsychology far more practical than it was in the earlier data-collection stage of research.

Nonetheless, science, particularly in the western world, retains the materialistic view that anything human which cannot be touched, tasted, seen, smelled or heard does not exist.

Even the development of advanced detection systems—which amplify the five senses—has not totally altered this point of view.

✖   ✖   ✖

The complete acceptance of psychic phenomena can only take place if science makes a concentrated effort to extend the rules of materialism to a point where they encompass the inner experience of mankind as well.

This can be accomplished by various means.

For instance, lie detectors and electroencephalographs assign specific numbers to mental states.

The ultimate aim of such an approach would be to determine enough quantities with regard to the physical activities of the brain to allow a specification of the internal human experience.

In brief, science's intransigent assumption of a one-to-one relationship between the brain and consciousness must be relaxed.

The actuality of psi phenomena can only be realized when science begins to question its conviction that all psychic function are tied to neural substance.

Jung himself claimed that the brain had nothing whatever to do with the psyche.

※　　※　　※

It is a matter of recorded fact that psi signals *run counter* to the principle of the decline of energy with the square of distance from its source.

Psi signals *are not impeded*—as customary energy signals are— by metal shielding—nor by hundreds of feet of water which are impenetrable to ordinary electromagnetic impulses.

No neural structure in the brain—or elsewhere in the human organism—has ever been discovered that could provide the large amount of energy required for long-distance transmission of psi symbols.

❊   ❊   ❊

Despite the continuing disparity of thought between science and parapsychology, progress (albeit halting) is being made.

Pieces of the continuing psychic puzzle are constantly being collected from all directions—and at an increasing rate.

The physical and the behavioral sciences are coming together.

Physics is blending with philosophy.

Biology with religion.

Medicine and engineering with literature and education.

In brief, a massive "cross-fertilization" is taking place all the time.

While it does, parapsychologists continue with a mass of laborious, repetitive testing, always intent on proving what they believe to be the truth of psychic phenomena.

No longer, in fact, do they regard their function as one of proving the occurrence of psi events.

They believe that this has already been accomplished.

What today's parapsychologists search for is *meaning.*

They know that psi exists.

Now they want to know *why.*

Afterword

On January 7, 1610, Galileo announced that, through his telescope, he'd seen four moons revolving around the planet Jupiter.

Immediately, a pamphlet was distributed by his enemies. *Nonsense*, said the pamphlet. Galileo saw no such thing. What he'd seen were halos; reflections; luminous clouds; in brief, an optical illusion. Worse, a self-delusion.

Accordingly, the Inquisition had its say and Galileo was compelled to recant.

Only in the past few years have they absolved him.

In 1807, Thomas Jefferson dismissed as utterly preposterous the notion that meteors could fall to Earth.

"It is easier" he said, "to believe that these two Yale professors" (who had examined the meteors) "would lie than that stones would fall from heaven." Earthly things could not fall from heaven.

Those peasants whose cottage roofs had been demolished by these meteors no doubt took a different view.

Of course these peasants were—unfortunately for the progressive course of science—not accredited as were the scientists who, in July of 1790, when a veritable *rain* of meteors fell on France declared it, quote, a physically impossible phenomenon, unquote.

In 1935, F.W. Moulton, one of the world's foremost authorities of celestial mechanics, did not hesitate to claim that "In all fairness to those, who by training, are not prepared to evaluate the fundamental difficulties of going from the Earth to the Moon, it must be stated that there is not the *slightest* possibility of such a journey."

We smile at such ignorance. But do we feel uneasy at the same time? How many truths of tomorrow are being attacked as the heresies of today? How many current Galileos will recant their observations? How many current meteoric concepts will be condemned as utterly preposterous?

Especially in the field of ESP.

※　　※　　※

Unhappily, the answer is self-evident. I have only to quote the scientist—still alive—who declared, of ESP, "This is the kind of thing that I would not believe in even if it existed."

Knowing this to be the case, it is all the more ironic that the founders of Parapsychology believed—with an almost majestic naiveté—that the scientific community would embrace them as soon as enough experiments had been carefully performed.

Yet here, more than a century later, Parapsychologists are still judged to be the loonies of the technological world because the phenomena they study contradict the "accepted" laws of the universe.

Consider the following quotation made by a well known—I will not identify him—critic of the field.

"In view of the *a priori* evidence against it, we know, in advance, that telepathy cannot occur."

Quoting further from the same distinguished source, "If the results could have arisen through a trick, the experiment may be considered unsatisfactory proof of ESP <u>whether or not is finally decided that such a trick was, in fact, used.</u>"; aghast underlining mine.

It is assumed to be the province of science to investigate nature without prejudice.

Nowhere has this dictum met with less observation than in the field of Parapsychology.

It is a fact that no other accumulation of evidence, attested to by so many people from all walks of life, has ever been rejected.

Unfortunately, Parapsychologists do not, in the eyes of science, qualify for this largess.

Indeed, Parapsychology has been called the "deviant" science.

Hopefully, recent developments call for a revision of this intransigent attitude.

In scores of university centers and research laboratories, there has been a compilation of experimental findings which can no longer be explained away as artifacts, statistical errors or the results of some bizarre, international conspiracy of fraud and collusion.

There has been a mounting number of observations involving apparent telepathic incidents in the psychotherapeutic world.

Finally, the attitude of modern physics is gradually altering in regard to the concepts of time and space and the heretofore, supposedly immutable laws of cause and effect.

In so-called "legitimate" science, the more that is discovered, the farther the horizon of knowledge recedes, the more underlying assumptions are discarded and replaced.

Conventional reasoning always fails us in the end. As Margaret Mead has stated, "The history of scientific achievement is full of scientists investigating phenomena the establishment did not believe was there."

Or, to quote the venerable *Encyclopedia Britannica*, "The history of science is partly the history of paradoxes becoming commonplaces and heresies becoming orthodoxies."

Would that the majority of today's scientists had, at the very minimum, the attitude of Thomas Edison who, when asked to describe electricity, replied "Don't know what it is. But it works."

Sadly, even that is an attitude rare.

Bibliography

Bartlett, Paile E., *Psi Trek*, New York: McGraw-Hill Book Company, 1981.

Blundson, Norman, *A Popular Dictionary of Spiritualism*, New York: The Citadel Press, 1961.

Brown, Slater, *The Heyday of Spirtualism*, New York: Hawthorn Books, Inc., 1970.

Carrington, Hereward, *Eusapia Palladino and Her Phenomena*, New York: B. W. Dodge and Company, 1909.

Carrington, Hereward, *The American Séances with Eusapia Palladino*, New York: Garrett Publications, 1954.

Carrington, Hereward, *Personal Experiences in Spiritualism*, London: T. Werner Laurie, Ltd., No date given.

Ehrenwalk, Jan, M.D., *The ESP Experience*, New York: Basic Books, Inc., 1978.

Ford, Arthur, *Nothing So Strange*, New York: Harper and Brothers, 1958.

Hintz, Naomi A. & Pratt, J. Gaither, Ph.D., *The Psychic Realm, What Can You Believe*, New York: Random House, 1975.

Helroyd, Stuart, *Psi and The Consciousness Explosion*, New York: Laplinger Publishing Company, 1977.

Knight, David D., Editor, *The ESP Reader*, New York: Castle Books, Grosset & Dunlap, Inc., 1969.

Lodge, Sir Oliver, *Raymond on Life and Death*, New York: George H. Doran Company, 1916.

Moore, R. Laurence, *In Search of White Crows*, New York: Oxford University Press, 1977.

Moss, Dr. Thelma, *The Probability of the Impossible*, Los Angeles: J. P. Tarcher, Inc., 1974.

Murphy, Gardner, *Challenge of Psychical Research*, New York: Harper & Brothers, 1961.

Rogo, D. Scott, *Psychic Breakthroughs Today*, Wellingborough, Northamptonshire: The Aquarian Press, 1987.

Somerlott, Robert, *Here, Mr. Splitfoot*, New York: The Viking Press, 1971.

Steinour, Harold, *Exploring the Unseen World*, New York: The Citadel Press, 1959.

Stern, Jess, Edgar Cayce, *The Sleeping Prophet*, New York: Bantam Books, 1967.

Sudre, Rene, *Para-Psychology*, New York: The Citadel Press, 1960.

Tanner, Amy E., *Studies in Spiritism*, New York and London: D. Appleton and Company, 1910.

Targ, Russell and Harray, Keithe, *The Mind Race*, New York: Villard Books, 1984.

Tyrrell, G.N.M., *Science and Psychical Phenomena plus Apparitions*, New Hyde Park, N.Y.: University Books, 1961.